New York Hustle

Pool Rooms,
School Rooms
&
Street Corners

"Maron's fascinating, compelling autobiography show-cases his smorgasbord of work-related experiences, his union involvement and changing attitudes, providing wonderful insights into the recent past."

Ray Walsh, *Lansing State Journal*

"…a moving and intense memoir…Maron's ultimate take-away is poignant: The past is like a cemetery; we can visit if we want or we can abandon it and let the weeds grow. But whatever mysteries lie beneath those headstones, we can't let them kill our dreams."

Eleanor Bader, *Review Fix*

"I did what I could to survive," he says, and so he did, dog-gedly resourceful, making his way not knowing where he was going but getting there nevertheless; from the very be-ginning, from babyhood almost, vividly and courageous-ly observant about himself and his own experience, and everyone around him, making his way, the foster home, the hapless schools, the street corners, the precarious jobs, seeing it all and all the people in it as he goes. The way he tells this story is a lesson in good writing and a lesson in courage and self-respect."

David Ferry, 2012 Winner
National Book Award for Poetry

"Read New York Hustle and become transfixed by the power and eloquence of the prose. From the shores of As-bury Park to the beaches and pool halls of Brooklyn, Stan Maron has written a superior memoir."

Joseph Trigoboff, author of *Rumble in Brooklyn.*

"Stan Maron tells it like it is and like it was to live the hard life of a hustler on the hardest of New York City streets.

Hear the truth from the man who knows the score."

New York Hustle

Pool Rooms,
School Rooms
&
Street Corners

by Stan Maron

HARDBALL

PRESS

New York Hustle - Pool Rooms, School Rooms and Street Corners, by Stanley Maron

Editing by Matthew Sheard
Cover and interior design by D. Bass
Published by Hard Ball Press.
Information available at: www.hardballpress.com
ISBN: 978-0-9911639-7-7

To Sally, Nina, and Greg
"May there always be sunshine"

Contents

Chapter 1: Belmar

My father and I never spoke much about personal matters until he was nearing his end. Our relationship always ranged from one of turbulence to estrangement. Maybe we just didn't trust each other. I never forgave him for a ride we took early one morning in his old maroon Chevrolet in 1938, when I was four years old. I remember it clearly.

That ride wasn't our usual Saturday morning drive to the farmers' market in a nearby town. Going to the farmers' market was a special treat for me. The road was long and curvy with trees on all sides and dogs tied to fences as we neared the crowded stalls. I loved the market, with its smell of fresh fruit and fresh cut flowers. We would often buy some nice ripe tomatoes and a basket of juicy apples that I always dug into the moment I could get my hands on one. I loved seeing men and women carrying children, wearing all kinds of colorful clothes, moving fast in every direction, passing money from one person to the next and talking in loud voices in languages I didn't understand.

I also enjoyed the ride to Rudy's, my Pop's car mechanic, traveling down a busy highway past all the stores and old houses. Rudy spoke with such a thick Yiddish accent I could hardly understand the words. It's been more than 70 years, but I can still hear my Pop and Rudy having a discussion on some mechanical issue. Pop swore by "Rudy the Mechanic."

The best ride of all was to my father's tailor shop, where I got to watch the men and women cut and sew the fabric and make new clothes. It was a boisterous, smoke-filled room full of loud machinery and cursing voices, better than a busy seaside boardwalk.

But that morning's ride in '38 was a different kind of journey; one with no fun. Just a short drive to the scary back room office of a guy who must have been a lawyer. The scary guy asked me only one question. "You want to go with Jacob and your brothers, don't you?" This was his version of custody law, and it worked on me. Even though I was experiencing feelings of betrayal and fear for not choosing to go with my mother, I wasn't able to place blame on any of the people in my life at the time. I knew something was wrong and I felt confused.

Where was my mother? Why wasn't she taking me with her? What would happen to our family? Nobody  explained what was happening to me. Since I was just a little boy, I probably wouldn't have understood them, anyway. It would be many years before I understood what had happened to my family, and even then, the mystery of my mother's fate would haunt me, wanting to know the truth about why she abandoned me. And even if the lawyer had told me why my parents were separating, at four years old, I couldn't have done anything about it.

Stan

The two brothers the lawyer was referring to were my half-brothers from my father's first marriage, Meyer, 18, and Hymie, 15. That marriage was never discussed in my presence. Meyer and Hymie were nice to me and made life bearable at the time. The house we had lived in on 3rd avenue in Asbury Park, New Jersey was lost because of a mortgage default, but that was a mere sidebar of the misery surrounding the breakup of my family. My pop blamed everyone and everything for the loss of the house except his gambling addiction, which was no doubt the main cause of the foreclosure.

Kate, my mother, also had a son and daughter from her first marriage, which had ended in a sloppy divorce. When the divorce was granted on the pretext that Kate was an incompetent mother, her two children, Eleanor, 8 and Julius, 10, were awarded to her husband. After a few days of having the children, her ex-husband, who must have been quite an asshole, brought them to the home of my mother's parents in Asbury Park and dropped them off with no explanation. I think he never wanted the kids in the first place, but used the custody as a ploy for the conditions of the divorce.

A year after my mother's divorce, my mother and father were introduced by a friend of my grandfather and were married a few months later. Eleanor and Julius, my mother's children, and Meyer and Hymie, and my mother and father moved into a house on 3rd Avenue in Asbury Park. When I came along a year later, we five children could be called a full house. Or maybe just two pairs and a deuce.

Hymie and Meyer

My mother's kids were only with her for the first two years of her marriage to my father. It was probably for the best. My father said they would be better off with my mother's parents, where they had lived after my mother's divorce. He was right. My mother's parents were kind hearted people who loved kids. Grandpa lost his fur shop in the 1930s during the depression. But he kept working from his home and made a pretty good living. Grandma always had a smile and a few cookies to keep the kids happy.

I have always felt short-changed in not having gotten to know Ellie and Julius better in my childhood years. But I really think they were lucky not having to hear the insane arguments and hysterical insults that took place with regularity between my parents, Jake and Katy. It also didn't help that we were living at the time of the Great Depression, when there just wasn't enough to go around on a tailor's salary, and for sure not a tailor with a serious gambling habit. Jake was addicted to any form of gambling, especially pinochle and poker. Somebody had to leave the house, and it wasn't hard for Jake to rationalize that it should be Ellie and Julius rather than his own children.

As a result of our visit to the lawyer, my parents separated and I went to live with my father and brothers. We moved into a boarding house run by Mary Rosen, who was the divorced wife of one of my father's card-playing buddies. The place she ran was a cross between a tragic drama and a carnival. She was an unhappy soul who seemed to have never gotten over her divorce, because all I really remember about her is that she kept up a continuous tirade on what a "no-good bum" her ex-husband, Charlie, was, and that she wished him no less than a "finstera yur", Yiddish for a dark future. Mary lived with her only child, six-year old Helene, and whoever the boarders were at the time, always fewer in number during the winter months than in the summer vacation season. The house was located a few blocks from the ocean in Belmar, a beach town on the Jersey Shore. When walking on the sand, I could see the high waves and smell refreshing clams—when they weren't rotting.

Helene's natural inclination was to be quite playful. Since Mary wouldn't allow her much freedom, Helene spent most of her time diapering and talking to her dolls. I felt jealous and left out of the scene. On one occasion, I snuck my face towel around one of the dolls and made the mistake of bragging to Mary about how I had diapered one of Helene's dolls with my towel. Somehow my father got wind of what I had done. He became furious and dragged me into our bedroom, saying in a loud, angry voice that, "boyess don't play with dolls unless dey are sissies" and that I should never play with dolls again. "Your brothers never playued with dolls." I think this was the first time in a lifetime of being reminded of what great sons my brothers were, and I should be just like them. But I wasn't.

Sometime during the busy summer season in my fifth year in life, I developed a strong interest in some of Mary's short-term guests. Her practice was to simply drape a curtain across a negotiated section of a room, which resulted in dormitory-style cramped quarters. I soon discovered that the curtains were thin enough to reveal some points of great interest to me, notwithstanding my severe nearsightedness. One family she rented to was especially colorful. Mary situated them in part of a front room where there were several windows, providing me with great visibility. Each morning the older child would accompany the younger child out of the room and walk in the street in the direction of the beach, only a few blocks away. The two older people, I guess the parents, would then move very close to each other, unclad in what looked to me like a great game. I didn't know what they were doing, but judging from what I was able to see and hear, it sounded like great fun.

My father and brothers never found out about my secret summer project. They couldn't, because by the time they got home from their night newspaper route, which Meyer had set up to make expenses for the upcoming school year, it was very late and always very quiet in the house. I was glad my new nameless friends were day people. In any event, I sure wasn't anxious to share my most stimulating discovery with anyone.

On a visit with my brother Hymie sometime around 2009, I told him the story of the couple in the front room and how I enjoyed watching and listening to them play their morning games. After hearing the story, Hymie had only one comment about my voyeuristic adventure. "Why the hell didn't you tell me? I thought all you learned that summer was when I taught you how to tie your shoes."

During our first summer at Mary Rosen's boarding house, Pop had just gotten his driver's license back after a one year suspension. He had been charged with hitting a dog and leaving the scene of the accident, even though he claimed to have given all the necessary information to the dog's owner. He even offered to help transport the animal to a veterinarian.

When Jake was close to 90, I visited him, along with my son, Greg, and my wife, Sally. During the visit I asked Pop to tell us his account of what happened when he ran over the dog, partly because I was curious and partly because I thought Greg would find the old guy entertaining. I didn't think Jake would mind reminiscing.

"What happened when you hit the dog with your car when I was a little boy, Pop?"

He looked around in his cagey style which he managed to hang on to all of his life until his death at 100 and said, "Oh, I just hit de dog and hurt his leg. The dog could valk

6

and I still offered to take him to de animal hospital but de owner said he would take him. He said I ran away. "He was a dam liar, dat sum da betch." Anyway I didn't want to be late for vork." We all laughed politely.

Greg, Sally, Stan and Nina

Apparently, the judge wasn't impressed with Jake's work ethic. "De judge fined me ah 100 dollars, dat bestard". None of us were ever clear on what really happened, but I do know Jake liked dogs. Hymie had also told me many years later that our Pop did try to help, but the owner refused. So the story hadn't changed through the years.

I liked the car my Pop bought after his license suspension was lifted. It was a late model, blue, second-hand Studebaker, which appeared very shiny and neat and made me feel great pride. After laboring all day in a coat factory, Pop was now able to assist as driver for Meyer and Hymie's paper route. He made sure that he got my brothers their papers in time from the distributor, Basil. I always heard talk about how my Pop and my brothers had to plan and outsmart their competitors so they could get out to the spots before the other paper boys. One of the spots they always talked about was Russ Vinton Farms, which was a famous night club haunt, where some folks even tipped the paperboy. I think that was their favorite spot. In a recent conversation with Hymie, I asked him about Russ Vinton Farms. He said they only went there on weekends and it was the only thing he liked about the whole paper deal. He joked, "Sex, drinking, dancing and money and none of it ever came my way: that was Russ

Vinton Farms in the late nineteen thirties."

Meyer, who was attending Cooper Union College, had set up the paper route to make expenses for the school year. Meyer was a highly motivated person who had very little time for anything but work. Although he was a good looking athletic type of guy, I remember him telling Hymie on one occasion that he didn't have time for some girl who had been flirting with him on his job. He worked all day at the Casino, which was an amusement center on the Asbury Park Board Walk. The Casino was a big place with a merry-go-round, all kinds of games and lots of machines where people could win prizes. It was the Jersey shore version of casinos, where gifts were won, as opposed to today's Atlantic City or Las Vegas, where gamblers can win real money. Some patrons won nice prizes if they were lucky at the games.

Meyer's job was supposed to be selling tickets for the rides and games, but when the manager saw what a good worker he was and how he often helped people who had faulty machines, he was promoted to be the mechanic. The casino job and the paper route allowed him about four hours of sleep each night.

Hymie, who was entering his senior year in high school, reluctantly contributed his labor to the paper route. It was clear to me even as a child that Hymie was not satisfied during that period in his life. He loved to read. Since Hemingway was his favorite writer, I think he wanted a life of adventure. When he sometimes complained about not getting paid for his work on the paper route, he was told in our father's typical form of reasoning, "vat do you need money for if you're not even in college yet?"

I liked going out on the paper route with them at the times there was nothing else they could do with me. It actually seemed like a lot of fun, plus the car was not a bad place to sleep. On good weekend nights there was even a bonus. After finishing the route, they would buy beer and pizza, and chocolate milk for me. I liked the beer better and managed to beg a fair amount of it, since at that hour my screechy holler and nasty 5-year-old disposition were no match for our gang.

When the summer ended, Meyer went back to Cooper Union and I missed him terribly. Hymie enrolled me in kindergarten class at the Belmar Elementary School. In school, we played games and learned to write letters and numbers. I always managed to establish these characters in a backward form, which amazed everyone. I think not being able to see the blackboard and maybe being a little dyslectic, as well as having a touch of Aspergers, had something to do with my backward lettering.

At this time Hymie, who was finishing his senior year in High School, had also passed the entrance test to attend Cooper Union College. With two brothers who had both handily passed the Cooper Union College entrance exam, one of the hardest and best college scholarships at that time, I've often wondered how two such smart guys couldn't surmise that I was half blind and had a learning disability. Go figure.

At the end of my kindergarten year, I was left back, a rare academic, historical achievement for one so young as I. The teacher tried her best to pacify me by awarding me a paper camel that all the kids had participated in making by placing strips of paper on a form until the camel was completed. Hymie picked me up at school that day. The camel made little difference as we walked home. I felt bad and cried a lot. Hymie tried his best to downplay the incident by finding me a real live turtle to keep my camel company, but I could see how disappointed he was in his little brother. I took some comfort knowing it was summer again, it would feel good to see Meyer when he came back home to resume making money for his next school year.

On Sundays, Hymie would ride me crossbar on his bicycle along Main Street through Ocean Grove to Grandma Gussie and Grandpa Jacob's house in Asbury Park. I liked being close to Hymie and felt comfortable and secure with him, even though the crossbar got a little hard on my rear end after a while. It was still something I looked forward to each week. At the time, Jews weren't allowed to live in Ocean Grove, but I guess riding on a bike through the town was okay as long as we didn't stop and get off our bike.

Eventually, we got to our destination. I remember one time my legs had fallen asleep from sitting still for so long. After dismounting the bike and taking one step, I fell down on my rear.

My mother would come in for the day from Highlands, New Jersey, where she worked as a domestic worker and also helped out in her sister's home, where she lived. During these visits to Asbury Park, my mother looked very sad and never spoke much. She often had tears in her eyes, which made me feel really bad. In searching my memory, I can't recall if I cried, too, but I am sure my mother was deeply depressed.

Hymie would take me to the door and say hello, but he would not enter the house. During this period of our family separation, I craved the togetherness of any form of bonding. I wanted my half-brother, Hymie, and his stepsister, my half-sister, Eleanor, both of whom I loved, to be close friends. I often fantasized how things might be different, but the hard feelings caused by our father, a very stubborn man, were the source of many of our problems. I know Hymie would have loved to have spent time with Eleanor. I think he loved her a lot. She was an exceptionally beautiful and smart high school sophomore at the time. She admired Hymie and would have liked to have spent some time with him on those visits, too, but it never happened. Hymie just told me what time he would be back to pick me up and disappeared.

Julius, Eleanor's brother, was also living with our grandparents. He was a lively fellow who liked rough horseplay, but was usually not at home on Sunday, always a disappointment for me. I didn't know at the time that he had quit high school and was waiting for orders to report to the Civilian Conservation Corp. The CCC Camps were set up during Franklin Delano Roosevelt's Administration in the 1930's. They were one of FDR's New Deal reforms and were success-  ful in getting a lot of young men off the streets and into worthwhile projects. It didn't work for Julius. I don't think anything could. He never seemed to be satisfied with what was happening in his life at any time that I can remember.

Ellie was a more serious type. She would sometimes take me for a walk and buy me ice cream. We would talk about school and cars and horses, which she loved, and what our future might be. I

Eleanor

always looked forward to the moment when I would see them all, even if it was a bittersweet occasion. For me, being at my Grandparents' on Sunday was different from the rest of the week. I think that Eleanor's charm and warmth made a big difference. Though we never had a chance to build a solid brother/sister relationship, I still felt good in her presence.

I once asked Julius what he was learning in the CC Camps. He answered, "To be a bum." I don't think this was the case for most young people who participated in the program, but his description no doubt fit him like a hand-made suit.

About a year and a half after my parents' separation, when we were still living at Mary Rosen's boarding house, Jake and Katie began seeing each other again. One night, I fell asleep as Hymie told me the story of Jack and the Beanstalk for probably the 1000th time (it was the only story he must have known). I woke up to find my parents standing at the foot of my bed, my father all dressed up and in a jovial mood and my mother with a sweet smile and tears in her eyes. It was like a dream. I remember my father asking me whether I would like for them to get back together again, as they kissed like a couple of lovebirds. I will never forget the warm feeling that came over me. That was the happiest day of my young life. I was sure all the bickering and shouting would be over at last.

Chapter 2: Asbury Park

A short time after my parents reunited, they reclaimed our furniture from storage and rented the ground floor of a house on Monroe Avenue in Asbury Park. The house was pretty nice. This was a good memory for me: my mother and father sitting together on our old sofa, the old wooden coffee table with the cigarette burn marks in front of them.

I could see the trains coming and going from my bedroom window and didn't even mind hearing the loud train-clanging noises, ringing bells and cinders when I walked near the tracks. It was a long walk to the beach. Our new neighborhood was considered on the wrong side of the tracks, but for me it seemed all right.

At first.

Our upstairs neighbors mentioned that the house had been constructed to house the Pennsylvania Railroad construction executives when the railroad was built in the 19th century. Not a bad move for a kid who had been living in rooming houses for the past two years.

It wasn't long before I found out that the kids on the block were real tough. Fist fights were part of the post-Depression culture. Some were bullies and some just liked to fight, no matter what the outcome. I heard some bad talk about President Roosevelt from some of the older kids, who called him a pinko. I didn't think his color made any difference, but I tried to limit my politics to marbles and tag games.

There was talk of my sister Ellie coming to live with us during her senior year in high school, but it never happened and she remained with my grandparents. I was very proud when she came to visit. When she left, my mother often went to her room and cried. But, looking back, I know it was a lot better for her at our grandparents' home.

My transfer from Belmar Elementary School to Bond Street Elementary School in Asbury Park should have been a routine transfer, but it turned out to be more of a three-ring circus, with me as the clown. After my mother and I entered the small, red brick schoolhouse and made our way to the Principal's office, we were interviewed by a person who introduced herself as the assistant to the principal. Soon after my mother handed the Assistant Principal my records from the school in Belmar, she was told that I would be placed back in a kindergarten class because I had not done well in the last school year. Upon hearing this assessment, I can remember a long silent pause, which was scary for me. I was pleasantly reassured when my mother began telling this person on the other side of the desk how smart I was and how well I was going to do in my new class. She raised her voice and flailed her arms in the air while breathing heavily and declaring repeatedly that the whole thing was an administrative mistake.

At this point, I don't believe I helped my mother's plea very much by jumping out of my chair and lunging out of the room and down to the end of the hall, where I made a sharp turn up a staircase and into one of the 2nd floor classrooms. I remember feeling rescued when my mother and the Assistant Principal, who were both in hot pursuit, reached the room where I was being restrained. It took a few minutes to quiet me down, at which point we returned to the office of the Assistant Principal.

My mother was in no mood to have anything more to

do with the Assistant Principal, who she blamed for getting me upset. She demanded to see what she called the "real principal." In no time at all, the Assistant Principal brought us to the Principal's office, where we were given seats and introduced to a tall, thin lady who seemed very serious and scary. My mother, having regained her composure, began talking very calmly about how a mistake is being made in wanting her very smart son to repeat kindergarten during this school year. She identified herself as the daughter of Jacob Reznick, who operated a small fur shop in town and had done work for many of the town school teachers in past years. My mother then got into a discussion of fashionable fur accessories, leading the Principal into believing that if she needed any fur work done, my grandfather would handle it at a handsome saving. Mother then proceeded to explain that I could make numbers and letters and would be well-behaved. The Principal seemed sold and placed me in the first grade. I always wondered whether she went to my granddad for any fur work, but I think if she did we would have heard about it. It was not uncommon for my grandfather's daughters to make promises that he felt obligated to keep.

My Grandpa on my mother's side was a tall guy also named Jacob, like my father. Grandpa gave the impression of being easy going, but he was brusque and stern with me. I don't think I was able to relate to him or, for that matter, to anyone at that time in my life. My father and he were not on good terms. I was told the bad blood had something to do with the loss of our house on 3rd Avenue before the family breakup. I know they had not spoken to each other since the early days of my parents' marriage. My father would always refer to my grandfather as a crook in a very hostile manner. Since my Grandpa was a successful businessman, there was probably some jealousy and a lot of other stuff involved in the estrangement. Anyway, as my mother and I walked home from school that morning, hand in hand, I was truly impressed and felt as if I were holding the hand of a conquering hero. She, too, was all smiles. Looking back, it seems as if we were two rubes at a country fair who had just won the big bunny.

Next on my agenda was enrollment in Hebrew school, a chore my father felt should be left to him. The Hebrew school was located in an old Jewish Community Center that had once been a Baptist church. It had the distinct smell of old moldy wood and had a deteriorating clapboard exterior, badly in need of a paint job. This Hebrew School was nothing like the after-school program in the reform synagogue on the other side of the railroad tracks in the more affluent residential district close to the beach. I had visited that school on a few occasions with my cousin, Arthur.

Inside the Hebrew school were about ten rooms, drably painted, one of which was the main classroom, a large room with many windows and about twenty-five small desks. There were three grade levels: beginners, middle, and Bar Mitzvah class. Each of the groups attended one hour a day, four days a week. Two hours on Sunday morning were allotted to Bible study. Although we were taught to read the Bible in Hebrew lettering, we were not taught the meaning of the words. I am sure that all of the kids trusted in what God had written and felt no need to check on him.

I found the oral translation of the Bible by our teacher, Mr. Reisman, interesting and reassuring. He was a very kind, strong man, always neatly dressed. He wore cool, gold-rimmed glasses. He told us how the Jews were the first to introduce the concept of one universal God, and that before this innovation, people had worshipped mere idols. This was a great boost to my self-esteem, since in my short time since arriving in Asbury Park, a couple of my new playmates had mentioned that the Jews had killed Jesus, who was God. I saw this as ridiculously silly and was sure that Mr. Reisman knew better. On one occasion I told him what one of the kids had said and asked for the real scoop. All I remember is Mr. Reisman laughing out loud as if the question was a foolish one. "Jesus was killed by the Romans," he said, "but they blame the Jews for everything."

My closest relationship at that time was with my brother, Hymie, who came to live with us after he dropped out of Cooper Union College, despite having a full scholarship. Cooper Union was founded by Peter Cooper. Cooper believed that anyone who was bright was entitled to a good education, regardless of their financial status. He was ahead of his time. I think Hymie felt he was educated enough and that his place should go to some other deserving individual. He told our father that he was not learning anything and the professors were boring. I think he just wanted something more stimulating than a classroom environment.

My other brother Meyer was now in his senior year at Cooper Union. When Meyer came home for summer break, he seemed quite satisfied with his Spartan lifestyle. I got this impression because he was always telling me about a place called Nedick's, where he could get an orange juice, donut and coffee for a dime. It made me wonder about lunch and dinner.

That summer, Hymie landed a job selling portrait photography on the Boardwalk in Asbury Park. He was paid on a commission basis for selling people the idea of having their picture taken as they walked on the Boardwalk. I spent a lot of time that summer on a Boardwalk bench watching Hymie ply his craft. He always dressed in neat, short-sleeve shirts and matching pants and looked like a very sharp guy to me. I discovered that when a pretty girl came by, he talked to her longer than usual. He had frequent dates, so I guess he was saying the right things.

Sometimes, when he was home, we would have long, interesting conversations. One time when our cousin, Willy, came to visit, we got into a big conversation about religion. I jumped right into the middle of the discussion, confident I knew a lot because on the past Sunday I had learned all about Moses from Mr. Riesman. I was impressed with Moses. I told them how great I thought Moses was because of the things he had accomplished as a leader of the Jewish people, like parting the sea so the Jews could escape from slavery, and getting the commandments from God.

Willy seemed to take issue with my literal interpretation of Biblical events. He went on a bit of a tirade about how the idea of miracles being performed by Moses or anyone else was old-fashioned, and how myths had started in ancient times to explain things that people did not understand, like low water tides, lightning, fire and death.

He dramatized his theory by illustrating vivid images of men holding forth on issues of importance such as death, plagues, and wars to large assemblies of people, who became followers. These leaders often became quite rich from their leadership and their story book interpretations of natural events. Willy stood up from his chair and impersonated a speaker, shouting, "Fellow countrymen, listen to me and learn the truth of existence on God's earth!" He said the people who gave the most convincing explanations became rabbis and priests and made claims of being able to communicate with God. At first, I was disappointed and I put up an argument, telling him that Mr. Reisman would not agree with him and that he was making this stuff up.

At this point, Hymie intervened and said we had to do more study on the subject before forming strong opinions and changed the topic, but not before asking me not to tell Pop about our discussion because, he explained, Pop would probably not understand. I was a little confused and felt as if I had just been inducted into some kind of secret society. But I felt good about my big brother allowing me to hang out with the big guys and even share secrets.

As the summer of 1940 was drawing to a close, I was preparing to enter the second grade at Bond St. School. Hymie's summer job as a photographer had ended. World War II was beginning in Europe as Hitler and his Nazi forces were on the move. The United States would enter the war imminently. I began to hear conversations between Hymie and my father about wanting our father to sign for him to join the Army Air Corps, since he was not old enough to join himself. Hymie kept saying that he wanted to fight the Nazis; that the Nazis were bigots and anti-Semites who wanted to conquer the world. My father said that Hymie was very young and needed more time to think these things over. After a great deal of resistance, Jake eventually signed for Hymie to join, putting a huge smile on my brother's face. I shared in his happiness and felt proud.

Hymie was stationed at a base somewhere in Louisiana. My mother, who had only gone through the 5th grade, wrote letters that were dictated by my father, and she always put something in for me. I looked forward to this letter-writing occasion and felt as if I was getting a great opportunity at communicating with my big brother, the soldier and my hero.

When Hymie came home for his first furlough after finishing basic training, he looked real neat in his pressed uniform, shiny brass buttons, and highly polished shoes. I loved when we hung out together and wanted to go everywhere with him, so that everyone in the neighborhood would see us. Hymie gave me a large box of pictures that he had taken while in training at Arial Photography School in Louisiana. I was inspired and impressed with the pictures, and I could tell that my enthusiasm made him feel good, even though they were mostly pictures of high mountains. Come to think of it, there were a couple of more interesting shots. I remember a few close-ups of the 1940's ice skating champion and movie actress, Sonia Henie, coming down the plank from a large ship. There was also one of a bunch of soldiers sitting on toilet commodes in rank formation. A few of the guys seemed a bit puzzled, but the others appeared happy while looking into Hymie's camera.

My job during that furlough was to polish his shoes each day whether they needed it or not, and he paid me well. Ten cents a shine, and usually a fifteen cent tip, which added up to what I learned was called two bits in Army talk. He even showed me how to play solitaire and blackjack, just like they played in gambling houses out West. Hymie also said that, since I was now in the second grade, I would be able to write him letters. He showed me how to start a letter. It was always the same. "How are you? I am doing fine."

When the last day of his furlough came, I walked him to the train station. As we walked, I remembered something we had discussed about the life of a soldier during wartime. Since World War Two had already started, he cut the discussion short when he saw how sad and concerned I became about this subject. But as we waited for the train I could not get the bad thoughts of war out of my mind. We hugged and kissed and I remember both of us with tears in our eyes as the train left the station. I waved to Hymie and walked home with fear for the future. Losing my big brother came into my mind, but it was too painful and I tried to think of other things.

That year I wrote Hymie often, always starting the way he had shown me. At first I was unable to do much more than the opening, but in time I learned to add things. I remember writing about a mutt that we had acquired from a man who my Pop and I met in a deli. The man told us about his dog having a litter of pups and asked if we wanted one. He invited us to his house, where we picked out a beautiful black pup with shiny hair and an overactive personality we named Buster. Pop put him in a bag and placed him in the pocket of his greatcoat, which I thought was very generous and caring. I had never seen this side of my father. Maybe it was something new, or maybe something that he had regained from out of the past. It felt good to me. We all loved Buster a lot.

Around this time my brother Meyer had graduated from Cooper Union. He was unable to land a job in his field of engineering, so he took a job as a truck driver for Bamburger's, a department store in Newark, New Jersey. He commuted to work while still living in the same furnished room in the city that he had rented while in college. I think he knew that the job on the truck was just temporary. I don't know why he couldn't get a job in engineering, but I think anti-Semitism might have been a factor.

When he came to visit us on some weekends, I always asked him questions about his truck driving job, but he never wanted to tell me much about it. I guess he thought that even discussing this matter was beneath his level. After all, here was a guy who had worked his ass off to get into one of the best engineering colleges in the country and winds up driving a truck, just as the Great Depression was coming to an end.

Soon after World War Two started, Meyer landed an engineering job at Fort Monmouth Army Base in New Jersey and came to live with us on Monroe Avenue. He was always kind and friendly, but we never had much time to speak because he was either working or studying. Although he had studied mechanical engineering at Cooper Union, he realized, after graduating, that he wanted electrical engineering as a career choice. He worked very hard on his own to master the conversion and was eventually successful as an electrical engineer, building circuits for military aircraft.

A few months after Meyer came to live with us, he was drafted into the Army. That same year, Julius was also drafted, which meant that I now had three brothers in the service of our country. At around this time, my mother raised the question of having Eleanor come to live with us during her senior year in high school. My mother pointed out that this had been agreed to when she and my father discussed getting back together. My father did not outwardly disagree, but when Ellie came to visit us to make preparations for the move, he expressed some negative ideas about my mother being very hard to live with. He said Ellie was "better off staying with our grandparents where she already was." I hated hearing that statement. How could he interpret the future? My mother had a job at the Army Base serving food and Ellie had a part time job in a retail store. It probably would have been better for Jake to have left. In the end Ellie didn't come to live with us.

This was a big disappointment to me that I did not get over easily. It brought on the biggest argument that I remember between my parents. I can still hear the abusive language and loud hollering and awful insults that took place that day. The argument ended with my mother running out of the apartment in tears and Pop yelling curses at her back. He was a big man with big, powerful hands. I was afraid he would strike my mother in the heat of their fight. As a child, I wouldn't have been able to defend her should he knock her down. That was a bitter pill to swallow: being small and powerless against a bully of a father.

After that big blow-up, things began to change for me. Looking back, I don't think I was able to communicate well socially and I never really found out why. I believe it had to do with my dysfunctional, roller-coaster family life.

The arguments grew more and more frequent, and they seemed louder and more violent. My father began to break things by throwing them against the kitchen wall. The crazed hollering was hard for me to decipher, but there was talk during the arguments about my mother having had a sexual affair with her brother-in-law during their breakup. During their separation, Kate had not stayed with Ellie and Julius at our grandparents' place. She had worked as a domestic for her sister's family in Atlantic Hylands, New Jersey. My father suspected that she had had an affair with her brother-in-law. Maybe this is where my father's accusation came from.

I remember my father shouting loudly that my mother was a "whore," while my mother shouted back about his gambling away all the money they had. The language they

Jake

used toward each other was unbelievable. They should never have been together. I think my mother and I were both afraid of my father going totally out of control as his fury raged on and on. He smashed dishes and pounded the kitchen table with his huge fist.

I saw a change in my father around this period of his life. He was morose and more irritable than ever. Perhaps it was his having two sons in the Military in wartime that put stress on him, but I don't think that was the main problem. Arguments were occurring more frequently, and his anger escalated each day. I didn't really understand what was happening and had never seen people act like this before. My parents were so busy fighting with each other, they barely had time to pay me any attention. I was alone with two crazy, violent adults, too young to get away.

I cried after each argument and hoped it would be the last, but it never was. The whole scene scared me and I felt I had no place to turn for comfort. I do remember one of the especially bad arguments that took place one day when my father came home from the shop for lunch. I was in the living room at the time and heard things breaking in the kitchen. When I walked into the kitchen, I saw glass bottles and some dishes broken on the floor and felt scared and maybe a little guilty, like it was my fault they were fighting. Then I saw my father strike my mother with his great hand. It knocked her back and brought tears to her eyes. I ran out of the kitchen and hid in my room, crying and trying not to hear the argument as it rose to a crescendo.

When my father left the house to go back to work, my mother found me in my room. We were both crying. She asked me if she had to leave, would I come with her this time. I, an eight year old, was too upset at the idea that my parents would separate once more to answer her. How could I choose?

Had I been able to speak, I don't think I would have said I wanted to go with her, and I think she understood that. The sadness that came over her face when I remained silent was something terrible. I am not sure why I didn't say I wanted to be with her, because I did want to have a mother. Maybe I was afraid I would not see Hymie and Meyer if I abandoned my father—a child's logic follows its own warped understanding of the world.

What was unusual about this fight was that Kate and I were crying together. For the first time I was not ashamed of showing her my feelings, as I had been in the past. I may have become used to not being with my mother during the separation and somewhat immunized. My mother and I never grew close, I don't know why. I do know that she had serious emotional problems in her lifetime. During the arguments, I remember watching her face and hoping against hope that she would not break down and burst into tears, but she always did. Somewhere along the line, I learned to accept it as a fact of life.

We never got a chance to speak, but I think she was a very troubled person. I wish I could have helped her. I know that her first divorce took its toll on her, and that living through the Depression didn't help. I think in a way, I longed for the good old days before the arguments, when they were still separated. Even when they seemed to have stopped the hostilities, there was still an atmosphere of uneasiness and distrust between them.

I think that mistrust rubbed off on me.

Chapter 3: The Lonely Child

After the summer of 1942, I entered the third grade, where I did poorly from the start. I was given a note by the teacher that said that she thought I needed eye glasses and recommended that I be taken for an eye exam. At first, my father dismissed this as some kind of foolishness. I think he felt embarrassed about the teacher having made this discovery. But eventually reason prevailed and my mother took me for an eye exam. A week later, my glasses were ready. The optometrist put the glasses on my face and told me to look at a picture on his wall. A new world opened up for me. It was amazing! Miraculous. I felt happy as I looked at my new discoveries. It was as if something or someone in the picture was going to jump out of the frame and become part of my life. I asked the optometrist to take the glasses off and put them back on again. It felt as if he was performing a magic trick.

I remember the look of apprehension on my mother's face when my father came home from work that evening and saw his little son with cool, silver-framed lenses. We were both afraid of his reaction, but he was supportive and said the glasses would help me to do better. My schoolwork improved a bit, though I never became a great student.

My third grade teacher's name was Miss Parker. She used a method of putting stars on the blackboard for good kids and checks for bad kids. My buddy, Georgie, a nice Greek kid who lived across the street from me, accumulated a fair share of checks, as did I. Whenever possible, I negotiated my way up to the blackboard and erased our checks. Most of the time, I got caught. Georgie got left back that year and I barely passed. I remember walking home with Georgie the last day of school before vacation. We both felt sad and tried to hide the tears in our eyes from each other.

On that day, I learned that school alone is not a true test of intelligence. I knew how smart Georgie really was from when we had made money together the summer before. We would go to the Boardwalk and gather salt water taffy as it dropped from the rolling machine. Georgie had an idea of setting up our own salt water taffy stand so we could make a lot of money. The machine was situated outside of a store on the Boardwalk. Our move had to be executed before the machine operator could catch us and chase us away. Georgie explained to me that by the time he got off the platform chair he was sitting on, we could have our pockets full and ready to make a fast getaway.

When we felt we had enough taffy, we went to an area where Georgie said there were a lot of apple trees. We picked some apples before being chased away by a woman who came out of a house and said if we didn't scoot real fast, she would call the police.

We set up our stand near where we lived on a couple of boxes that we found near the railroad station. Georgie said he picked it because there were a lot of people passing by all the time. Georgie's mother helped by giving us a pitcher of lemonade, which we marketed at the bargain rate of 3 cents a cup. When we did really well selling apples, taffy and lemonade, I felt good. I was proud of us; we were successful business men. I mean, business children.

I remember a guy with a sharp suit and a nice lady coming up to our stand and asking for two lemonades. As they drank, the lady said "This is good" and the guy nodding in approval as he asked with a big smile on his face, "What are you? Jews?" I answered, "I'm a Jew" and Georgie said "Greek." The guy looked at the lady and said with a laugh, "Look what we have here, honey, a Greek and a Jew already making money."

But then my friendship with Georgie suffered a serious setback. I think Georgie's dad put the blame on me for his son's school problems and didn't allow Georgie to spend time with me during the rest of our summer vacation. I felt guilty and wished that we could be friends again, but it didn't happen. I missed the money we made, too.

That summer was my introduction to childhood misery. My brother, Hymie, was in the Air Corp, Julius and Meyer had been drafted into the armed services, and my mother had a job working in the cafeteria at Fort Monmouth Army Base in Long Branch, New Jersey. Left pretty much on my own, I was lonely and did not make friends. I used to go to a playground and ride the swings and see-saw. I also enjoyed pitching horseshoes, which I became pretty good at, but whatever family life I had was gone, and it hurt. Occasionally, I walked to my grandparent's house, where I knew I could always get a good hot meal and be near family. They lived on Summerfield Avenue, which was located on the nicer side of town, and I liked to go there. My Grandma Gussie was very good natured. I wish I had gotten to know her better. I didn't see them too often, though, after my parents got back together.

Though I did not talk much with my Grandpa, I admired him. I think his strength and self-assuredness made me feel secure in his presence. He conducted his fur business in the attic of his home, equipped with safes, sewing machines, and a cutting table. During the busy season, he sometimes had a helper, but usually worked solo. He used the downstairs living room as his showroom. I would sometimes listen to his charming sales approach, especially with older women. He had a reputation for being a very sharp businessman. Most of his customers seemed to trust in him, even though my father always spoke in a nasty way whenever he referred to my grandfather, calling him a crook. My brother Hymie did tell me that one of the things that led to my parents breakup when we lived on Third Avenue in Asbury Park was that, when my father could not keep the mortgage payments up and the house where we were living was foreclosed, my grandfather would not help make the mortgage payments. My father never got over that refusal to help him.

I know that my father's gambling was at the heart of his financial problems and the bad feelings that came from them. In those days, many of the Jewish fathers and uncles I met seemed to be heavily involved in some form of gambling. My grandpa Jacob limited his gambling to real estate speculation and the fur business. I guess he knew what he was doing, because he got pretty rich in his later years. I blame my father for ruining my relationship with my grandfather, who provided a strong, no-nonsense role model for me; one I think made some difference in my life.

His wife, my Grandma Gussie, was a sweet, simple woman who was always gentle and nice. I don't know why we had almost no relationship other than her feeding me when I came to the house. I really think I had some form of extreme shyness or some disorder, like Aspergers. Anyway, whatever home life I had at the time was provided by my grandparents.

Walking around the neighborhood was one of my favorite pastimes. I made friends with an older man named Paulie, who worked at the railroad track crossing on the corner from my house. Paulie told me I should never back away from a fight. He taught me how to throw punches called jabs, straight rights, crosses, and hooks. As a result of his training, I got my ass kicked many times. I never wanted to fight, but in my neighborhood it was a means of survival.

I don't think my father ever thought much about the neighborhood we lived in except that the rent was cheap. But I was the only Jewish kid in the area. I knew this because I got to know where the kids from my Hebrew school lived. One of the things that I heard many times from kids and even adults was that the Jews had started the war, but were not fighting in it. When I asked my father about this, he told me that it was a lie. We decided to go downtown and purchase a banner with three stars: one for each of my brothers who were serving in the military. These banners were customary at the time. I didn't hear much about the Jews starting the war any more, but the bigoted nastiness and name calling still occurred on a regular basis. Kids pick a lot up from their parents and it's not all good. New Jersey was a Ku Klux Klan stronghold in the 1940s, and it hit hardest in the poor sections of the towns.

One time while playing near the railroad tracks, some men came up to me and asked if I was Jewish. They must have been tipped off by someone. A few days later a couple of old guys came up to me near the railroad tracks again and, as one held me down, the other put tar on my arms. He sent his friend to retrieve feathers from a butcher shop around the corner on Main Street. This tar-and-feathering terrified me, but I didn't really know what was happening. I do remember hearing these men utter some bad names, like "dirty Jew" and "little Jew bastard."

As I walked home crying, covered with the tar and the feathers, a man called me from his porch. He told me to sit down and wait a minute while he went to get a liquid solution, which must have been kerosene or something like it. He washed my arms and I sure felt better. That day I learned that there are those who will do bad things and those who will undo bad and give comfort to a stranger.

I had a lot of problems that summer. My falling out with my buddy Georgie didn't help things at all. It became more difficult to hang out with the kids on the block; I was definitely not well-liked. Georgie had many brothers and sisters who stuck together all the time. Once I had a fist-fight with Georgie and it ended in a pretty even way. We each had bloody noses and I had a swollen eye. I was at a serious disadvantage because I had to take my glasses off and find a place to put them, as Paulie, the railroad gate guy, had taught me to do. I know I gave up a lot with my sight handicap. After this fight, one of Georgie's big brothers began picking on me and I stood up to him at the cost of taking several bad beatings.

Not long after, one of the other kids, Gene Garrity, got the idea that I could be used as a punching bag. I had to fight him. Since he was older and bigger than I was, that bout didn't work out too well for me, either.

I never told my parents where the black eyes and puffed up facial swellings came from, but my Dad did know that I was fighting. On my part, I tried to keep some distance between me and some of the bullies on the block, but it wasn't always possible. I heard so many times from Gene Garrity that the Jews had killed God that I thought that was all they taught in Catholic school. One of his older brothers was a bit more creative. He liked to taunt me with what must have been his favorite chant: "Matzos, Matzos, two for five, that's what keeps the Jews alive, that's all they eat is Matzos and Gefilte fish."

In any event, I was already unmanageable: I listened to no teacher, parent or adult neighbor. I remember feeling bad all the time. It was like a wet soggy feeling inside of me that made me feel dirty and uncomfortable, while at the same time scared of the beating that was waiting for me whenever I left the house.

I have never dealt much with psychotherapy. Back when I was a child, therapy was only for the well-to-do neurotics, not depressed children like me. Maybe my personal troubles can best be summed up by growing up in a chaotic, sometimes violent, dysfunctional family, and living in an environment that was hostile to Jews. Maybe it was coming from a broken home with no real parenting. It all resulted in producing a nasty little bastard named Stanley.

But to be fair and not too maudlin, I did manage to make a few friends during that summer. One kid I met in the park named Billy Shire lived a few streets away from me. I liked him a lot, and we got along well. He wore a white sailor's cap that I thought was very spiffy. I got one and he showed me how to shape it. We would go to the beach together or to Walter Reade's Monty Carlo swimming pool. Billy used to come to my house and we would eat huge amounts of apples and tomatoes from baskets that my father had bought at the farmer's market.

One day I went with my mother and father to visit one of their friends. I mentioned that I had a friend who lived a few houses away from the people we were visiting. I said his name was Billy and his father was in the Navy. The woman we were visiting asked if I was talking about Billy Shire, while she laughed mockingly. "His father? He has no father," she said. As far as I was concerned, Billy's father was still in the Navy. I was convinced that my parent's family friend was an idiot. I left her house that night determined to find out.

The next day I asked Billy about where his father was stationed. He recounted that he had not seen his father since moving to New Jersey from Virginia, but that his mother and he were going to visit him soon on the base where he was stationed. I didn't ask where the base was. That was good enough for me. I went straight home and told my mother her friend was full of crap. My mother seemed to agree and said no more on the subject.

When summer ended, I went back to school. My parents were arguing a lot and had become more abusive than ever toward each other. The language and behavior was unbelievable. I felt there was no way out of their nightmare home.

The one thing that made me happy was that Hymie was scheduled to come home for his second furlough. The morning after his arrival, a bad fight took place between Jake and Katie. I was wishing that Hymie would not be subjected to this stuff, but I did see him wipe tears from his eyes over our parents' combat. I didn't want to cry in front of him. I wanted to act tough like I did in the street facing the anti-Semites, and I did manage to keep the tears in.

We had a lot of discussions during Hymie's furlough. He treated me more like an adult. A few days after a big fight between Jake and Katie, I remember him asking me how often these arguments took place. I broke down and started to cry, even though I was trying hard not to. We both felt bad. The feeling of all-pervading helplessness that I experienced probably left me with more than a few scars. I think the worst part of it all was the feeling of confusion about why these fights were happening so often.

On the last day of my brother's furlough, I walked with him to the train station, as I had done before, and cried when he departed. We corresponded regularly after his furlough. I learned he had volunteered for aerial gunner's school. He looked forward to being sent into combat when he completed his training. Unfortunately, a bad accident occurred at gunnery school. One of the guys training with him forgot to release the gas in one of the training gun's compression chambers as he was supposed to do. Hymie was burned in his face. After a couple of weeks in the hospital he was back on duty, but never got into combat as he had wanted.

My schoolwork had improved a bit, partly due to Hymie's talking with me about the importance of learning something useful. Thanks to his encouragement, I began to feel a little better about myself, despite the difficulties I was encountering at home and on the street.

Chapter 4: The Factory

My father decided that on days that I was not scheduled to go to Hebrew school I should go to the shop where he worked and help him. He would give me little chores, like turning the collars of the coats after they were sewn by the collar makers. The instructions for "pucking collars," as Jake said, was to "puck de corners straight, but not too hard and don't make ah hole in de goods." This meant that since the collars were sewn on the inside of the goods, the collar had to be turned inside out before being sewn, and the corners had to be "poked" with a long rod before they could be sewn by the operators and connected to the coat. Since machine operators worked on a piecework system, they were always glad to have me help them get the collars fast.

I liked the excitement and rhythm of the factory. I can still hear the loud hum of the sewing machines as the operators handily pushed the goods under the automatic needle, stepping hard on the machine peddle while focusing their eyes on the seams like laser beams. All this while regaling the worker on the next machine with the achievements of one or more of their kids.

One lady who worked on a machine was named Mamie. She had a nice, soft, singsong Italian accent and never stopped talking. On one of my visits to the shop, she must have told me five times about how her son, while playing for Neptune High School, blocked the kick in the big Thanksgiving football game, which led to Neptune winning by one point against Asbury Park, my hometown team. "My sonna Joey, hes a gooda boy and gets high marks in school and he's a football player. Last week at the big, big game he blocked the kick and Neptune High School won by one point. He's great."

I got a kick out of her boasting, while the delicious salad she treated me to made her one of my favorite people.

Making coats was a complicated operation. First the raw goods had to be stretched out by cutters like my father and his partner, Whitey. The goods were placed and stretched on a table about 35 feet long and 25 or 50 layers high. In the trade this was known as 25 or 50 high.

The material was marked with chalk around the paper patterns, which represented the different sections of the coat. The cutter then operated a hand machine. The goods had to be handled in a very careful and delicate way so as not to move any of the goods on the stacks. A fraction of an inch slip could mean a lot of waste, and goods were a costly commodity. My pop was a master cutter who could sew and press as well. He prided himself on being what he called an "all-around mechanic."

The goods were then moved where they awaited distribution to the sewing machine operators. Floor boys ran from machine to machine, carrying the stacks of cut goods and delivering bundles of backs and fronts, sleeves and collars, pockets and linings to the next operator whose work was running low. Some operators could only sew certain sections; some could do any section. Those who could work all sections were master operators and got the most work.

God help the floor boy if an operator ran out of work before he brought the next bundle. It meant money, and they were used to sustaining an uninterrupted work rhythm. The floor boy ran the risk of being cussed out in any one of ten languages, maybe all of them. I can still see my father's buddy, Urka, who was a presser and the last to get the finished product from the operators. If he needed coats and had to wait, you could hear him hollering and jumping. I have been told that at these times his language was limited to Russian curse words. I remember Whitey once telling him to "shut the fuck up", and that the coats don't grow on trees.

Every skilled worker in the factory at that time worked on a piecework basis, meaning they were paid by the number of garments that they worked on, so they sure didn't like work time being wasted. I think for the most part they got along well. Overall, the shop had a friendly feeling, so I liked hanging out there.

I loved the hissing of the steam of the big pressing machines as the bare-chested pressers wiped pouring sweat from their faces while chugging water or other liquid refreshments. What I was doing could have been considered child labor, but it kept me out of trouble, and I learned a lot.

Whitey was a character. He weighed about 90 pounds. His long gray hair was slicked back. He wore sharp white-on-white shirts and good suits, and he always had a cigarette hanging from the side of his mouth. He loved Jewish idiomatic expressions. He was of German Catholic background, but seemed to love Yiddish expressions like "shmuch" or "putz" (body parts), "michuga" (crazy) or "vergeharget" (drop dead). I always thought Whitey was the funniest guy in the world.

A couple of times Jake brought me to the Saturday afternoon poker game at the shop, where I got to see Whitey really act out. Usually after a few drinks, he would start picking on people for making what he considered bad poker plays, causing him to lose a pot. "The Shmuck should have folded when I raised!" Instead, the other guy stayed in and won the pot. "What a lucky putz." Jake never let me stay long, but when I was around I always got an earful and wasn't shy about sharing the stories with the kids at Hebrew school.

Then there was Gene the foreman, who seemed to be just walking around the shop assuming an important aura like a big shot. From time to time he would pick up a coat sleeve or a back and just look at it. Sometimes I could hear him telling an operator to "speed it up." Most of the workers seemed to act friendly when he spoke with them. Once I asked my father to tell me what Gene the Foreman did. His answer was to the point. "He don't do notink. He's ah dummy. Dats vy he's ah foreman."

Pop explained to me that the boss wanted to have a foreman to watch the production, but the union contract called for him to be a union member, so they agreed on Gene. I was left kind of confused on that issue. On another occasion I asked how Sam became a boss and how he became the shop owner. Pop's answer to that question was that he was the boss because he didn't know how to work. "He vasn't a good mechanic." Looking back I don't think my pop much believed these explanations, but he had a need to prop his self-esteem up. Maybe he was also half joking.

My pop was the union delegate at the shop and commanded the respect of the workers. One time there was a dispute which wound up in a fistfight between two pressers. The boss's son, Lou, a loud mouth who liked to act like a dictator, fired both pressers on the spot. Some of the people who were working near the incident came to my father and told him what had happened. Pop walked up to Lou and with his usual commanding voice said the men could not be fired without a union hearing.

My father agreed that the two men could be sent home

temporarily. An argument started between my father and Lou. Lou became abusive. My father walked around some of the machines and over some of the bundles of unfinished coats to where the main power switch was located and shut down all the machines in the factory. The shop became as quiet as a library. At this point Lou came running at my father with clenched fists. There were a couple of pairs of scissors on a nearby table. One of the women machine operators knocked them to the floor so that they could not be used in the fight. I was really scared and thought of jumping in to help, but was totally overwhelmed by the whole scene.

Although Lou was ten years younger than my father, they were both big bulky men. I didn't know what was happening as my father grabbed Lou's shoulders, pulled him forward and delivered a staggering head butt. As the workers separated the two, Lou threatened to break my father's head. My father replied in his best Yiddish-American accent, "You can kiss my ess." Fifteen minutes later, the two pressers had not been sent home and were back to work at opposite ends of the pressing section of the shop, and all was normal. A bit of good-natured ribbing went on at the time clock at the end of the work day. I remember one of the guys telling my father that he had a good head on his shoulders. One of the women quipped, "That Jake made good use of it today."

As we walked home that evening across Main Street past the railroad tracks with the darkness fast approaching, I could hear the autumn winds rustling a happy tune. Trudging through crispy brown leaves, I felt full of pride and asked my father where he learned to hit with his head. He said that when he was a small boy in Czarist Russia, he used to have fights with some of the kids who were anti-Semites, and he learned that from them. I was impressed and asked him to show me how to do a head butt. He just laughed, which was his way of saying that fighting is not good.

At this point in our lives, my Dad and I seemed to become a little closer. But most of the time my feelings of affection toward my father were cut short by events which were beyond my control. I liked walking home from the shop with him at the end of the day. While we sometimes had exchanges about things that were happening, we always steered clear of family matters. He sometimes liked to talk about Hymie and Meyer, and I would talk about my letters to Hymie and how he was doing. I think we both wanted to talk about our personal feelings, but I was ashamed and maybe even put part of the blame for the family problems on myself. I don't know why; I guess that's how kids react.

One day, we had barely left the shop when Urka, the presser, shouted at us from behind. When Urka caught up with us, he and Jake got into a conversation which I couldn't understand because they were speaking in Russian. Eventually, Urka pulled a bottle out of his jacket pocket and offered my Dad a drink from the bottle. At first my Dad refused, but Urka insisted. My Dad obliged and they both took swigs the likes of which I have never seen. I think Urka had a little head start on the drinking that day.

Urka then insisted that I take a drink from the bottle. We all started laughing as my Pop put a drop on his finger and touched my lips. I didn't really get much of a taste, but it sure smelled strong, just like rubbing alcohol. Urka offered Jake another drink, but Jake refused, saying, "de boy vil get drunk from de fumes." We all laughed as Jake and Urka shook hands and wished each other "Dobre outré" (Good night).

I think Jake was just plain sad about his marriage to

my Mom. He did begin to speak to me more freely about the War and my school work and how Eleanor was doing. Maybe the shots with Urka had a little to do with it, but Jake did open up a bit more than usual on our walk home that evening. He even took my hand, which made me proud to be sharing a walk in the winter cold with my Dad.

The worst part of it was that there never seemed to be any prospects of things getting better at home. I can almost say I didn't want the walk to end, for fear that something nasty might happen as soon as Pop stepped in the door and confronted Mom.

Chapter 5: The Little Money Collector

At Hebrew School things were really boring, until one day our teacher, Mr. Reisman, gave us little boxes with slits to collect money for the Jewish National Fund. He explained that this money was to be used to establish a Jewish state in a land that was now called Palestine. One afternoon I took the box to my father's after-work hang-out, the back room of a small restaurant where he and his buddies played pinball and cards for small stakes, and sometimes on weekends for not such small stakes. The restaurant was operated by his friend, a man named Mike Faro, the Democratic Party chairman of the ward, who doubled as a numbers bookie. Mike had contempt for the Protestant hierarchy who were in control of New Jersey politics. He was never shy about the language he used to describe these politicians he considered highbrow snobs. Although Mike never said much to me, he loved to tease me by telling me "your face is as round as the moon" and asking me why this was. My father once ribbed him back by telling him "your ass is as big as the moon." Mike's wife, Mary, who did all the cooking in the store, never had much to say, but on this occasion she laughed real loud. Mike seemed pissed and we all laughed with her.

At first my father didn't know what to make of my un-announced arrival, but when I brandished the collection box while talking it up for the Jewish state, it became clear to all. He fervently requested that his buddies kick in, and they did.

This worked so well that I made a second appearance

at the shop a few days later, where I urged Jake's co-workers to give until it hurt. As I walked around the sewing section and through the pressing section, I did well for a kid who was shy. I think that our Hebrew teacher Mr. Reisman gave us such a motivational pep talk that I was like a little fundraiser on steroids. It worked.

Jake helped by making a personal appeal to the bosses, saying, "You guys are making money and I know you support the people who are struggling to build a Jewish Homeland where dey will be safe and secure. You should give vith an open hand and an open heart and I know you vill and I vant to thank you."

Again the collection was a success. Even the boss's son, Lou, who my Pop had the fight with, gave some big bills, which impressed me so much that I hugged him and my Pop shook his hand for the first time since the fight had occurred.

After appealing to all of my personal contacts, I stationed myself on the corner of Main Street and Cookman Avenue, the busiest corner in town, where I began my public appeal, which commenced the last leg of my fundraising campaign. That year I collected the most of any kid in the whole school and was awarded a gold medal with a ribbon by some big time Zionist leader who came all the way from New York City to present the awards to the Jersey kids. My parents were very proud of me and bragged to everyone, and if they missed anyone, I sure didn't.

Soon after this period, things began to go downhill in my life. Fast. I was on an emotional roller coaster and was frightened all the time. My parents were getting into more fights at home, and I was getting in more fights in the neighborhood. My brother Meyer had been placed on some type of essential military project with the signal corps; something to do with decoding electronic data. I never found out much about it and I am not sure what it entailed. Meyer was always a closed-mouth, no-nonsense type of guy who carried an aura of mystery in everything he did. I did not see very much of him during the war, so I figured he was working on some super-secret spy operation that he couldn't tell me about.

Julius was in the Army too, serving in Europe. I had heard that he was okay, but we were not in touch. Hymie was stationed in Louisiana. Although he was not too far away, I wasn't writing to him much anymore. At nine years old I was starting to lose interest in everything and everyone around me, and I didn't really understand what was happening to me. With Hymie away in the army, I felt like I had no support from any one; as if I were hanging out on a loose limb.

My sister Ellie was working as a stenographer for the government and was doing a lot of traveling. I missed her and was glad to see her when she came home for a short vacation in the summer of 1943.

During this summer vacation, my mother had purchased tickets for herself and Eleanor to attend a Broadway show in New York City. My Mom left the house early that morning. I wasn't feeling well, and later in the day I became very sick. My father called a doctor to the house, who prescribed a powder medicine. My father instructed me on how to take the medicine with juice and went to

Stan's mother Kate
and Eleanor

work. It was crazy for either of my parents to have left me alone in the house, but they did.

I must have taken the medicine improperly, because I remember having hallucinations about the house caving in. When I tried to run out of the house to save my life I kept falling down.

The next day I was worse and could not move my leg. I was taken by ambulance to the hospital. As I was carried past my parents' bedroom, I noticed my mother in her bed. As I was carried down the front steps of the house, our dog Buster, who was tied to the rail, attempted to lunge at me in a show of affection. I had some pain in one leg and couldn't move it; I think the medication had done something to me. I remember being in pain and feeling sleepy and groggy and scared as I was placed into the ambulance. There was also a police car parked in front of the house, which I did not understand at the time.

I was admitted to the Fitkin Hospital. As soon as I arrived I remember a group of people in a circle standing around my bed talking to each other. I could tell from the conversations that they did not know what the problem was. They asked me a bunch of questions, but I don't think I had much information to offer them.

My father visited daily, but my mother did not come. When I asked for her, my father told me that she had eaten something bad on her trip to New York and had become sick. My sister Ellie visited one time and appeared withdrawn. She was not as talkative as she usually was. I sensed that something was not right and that I was not getting the full story.

On the fourth or fifth day, my father told me my mother was in a hospital. I told him I thought she was dead, but he denied it. After a week my leg got better. I was discharged from the hospital and brought to my uncle's house. I knew something was wrong, not being allowed to go home, but was afraid to ask.

The first evening at my uncle's house, my father and Meyer, whom I hadn't seen in a long time, went out to sit on the porch with me. My father then broke the news to me that my mother was dead. He said she had died of a heart attack the day that I had been taken to the hospital. I felt strange about this whole episode. It was unreal, like a dream. I shed a lot of tears in sorrow and frustration.

Since my mother had never been a sickly person, the story my father told me didn't add up. I do know that my mother was sick on the day I was taken to the hospital, which was the day after she had gone to New York with Ellie, because I had looked into her bedroom and seen her in bed when they were taking me out of the house to the ambulance. The excuse my father gave that she had eaten something bad in New York didn't sound right to me.

Nobody could tell me the reason for my mother's death. When I was taken to the hospital with my paralyzed leg, there had been a police car outside our home, not just an ambulance. What did that mean? My father was a violent man; I had seen him hit my mother more than once, and he often threw dishes and other things at her. And his unwillingness to tell me anything about her death added to the mystery.

The thought that he may have hurt her – may have been responsible for her death – haunted me then, and continued to haunt me as my childhood passed into adolescence.

I know my father had a bad temper and was high-strung. I think he had been angry at my mother for going to New York on the previous day with Eleanor. I have thought about my mother's death often. She was only 42 years old, slightly over-weight, but not an unhealthy person. I like to remember, and think of my father as a compassionate person, but I have always found his relationship with my mother extremely hard to reconcile in my mind. The element of not knowing something that was important in my life has never left me. As a child, my mother's sudden death haunted my dreams and cast a pall on my days.

I wanted to know the truth, but Pop wouldn't talk about what happened. It would be many years before I came closer to the truth about that terrible day.

Chapter 6: Out of the Frying Pan

About a month after my mother's death, my father arranged for the two of us to move into a boardinghouse on Main Street in Asbury Park, run by Mrs. Rauch, a Jewish lady of German background. The landlady liked to tell me how fine and cultured the German people were. And she bragged about her handsome son, who was a businessman in Hawaii. It was 1944, I was ten years old, with an argumentative personality already in full bloom.

"Hitler is a German," I told her.

She informed me that Hitler was not typical of the German people, but I didn't give her explanation much weight. She asked what my favorite dish was. When I told her it was spaghetti and meatballs, she cooked me the most delicious meal of my favorite dish every Sunday afternoon. I can still remember the taste of the tomato sauce with its biting garlic-scented flavor. I looked forward to eating large portions week after week.

Our landlady usually had three or four rooms rented at any given time, but I was the only one she cooked for. Some of her roomers seemed interesting and though I didn't get to know them well, one woman boarder named June was very friendly. June always asked me how things were going. She had long brown hair and was tall and pretty. One day she told me she was getting married and would be moving out soon. For a while, I missed seeing her around, but soon forgot her. I didn't get close to people at all during that period in my life.

There was a small store with a soda fountain on the

ground level just below our room where the jukebox and pinball machines were in constant use. I must have heard the song "Five Dozen Roses" 5,000 times, as well as "Give Me Five Minutes More." Sometimes I would be enjoying the music when the loud noises from the pinball machine would interrupt. These two devices, along with occasional loud arguments between the pinball players, made it hard to get to sleep at night. Luckily, things quieted down around 10 o'clock.

I made friends with a kid named Jackie, who I knew from school. He lived in a nice house and told me that his father had his own business, which impressed me. Once, as we were playing with a pinball machine he had in his basement, I saw his father folding a large amount of nicely pressed cotton dress shirts. When I began to ask his Pop questions about the shirts, he told me not to worry too much about the shirts. I related the story to my father, who told me the guy must be in the black market business. This was during World War II, when goods of this high quality were hard to come by and commanded a high price in what was called the "under the table" business. At this point, my father gave me a little lecture about keeping my mouth shut and not asking too many questions. He said I should learn to "mind my biss-ness."

Jackie gave me a pair of ice skates and we went skating together almost every day when the lake was frozen. We became good friends. I even ate at Jackie's house a couple of times, always remembering not to ask any questions about his Pop's business.

Before Jackie gave me the skates, I had gone to the lake every day and just slid on the ice without skates. Having my own skates was more fun. One time I fell in the lake near the shore line where the ice was thin, but the water was shallow. My corduroy brown pants got soaking wet.

As I rode my bicycle straight home, my pants froze on the way. When Mrs. Rauch noticed the frozen pants, I told her what had happened. She put the pants on the line to dry. I looked out the window while I was eating supper and saw the pants were frozen stiff.

I didn't want her to tell my father, but she did. That night, as I was getting ready to go to sleep and before my father went downstairs to the store to play pinball with some guys, he said he wanted to talk with me about what happened at the lake. He was angry and told me a lot of stuff about how bad I was and at one point said, "You killed your mudder and now you vant to kill me."

I answered, "I didn't kill my mother, you did!"

He got a terrifying look on his face; I could feel his anger. He said, "If you ever say anything like that again I'll wrap you in a blanket and throw you in the ocean."

I felt scared and knew I had said the wrong thing. That was the last time I ever felt any closeness or love for the man. I didn't touch on the subject of my mother's death again until many years later.

About a year after my mother's untimely death in 1943, it was becoming obvious to Mrs. Holt, my 5th grade teacher at Bond Street Elementary School in Asbury Park, that I wasn't acting right. But then, neither was she. All she ever talked about was how many "Japs" her son Chauncey, who was in the Marine Corps and serving in Guadalcanal, had said he killed in his last letter to her. She never taught much, but she convinced me and I think everyone else that the reason we were winning World War II was all because of Chauncey. At first I found this stuff entertaining, but as the year progressed, it began to get on my nerves.

Anyway, the highlight of my school day was talking to

Dinah during our classroom milk and crackers break. Dinah was a beautiful Gypsy girl who sat behind me. She always told me entertaining things on days when she came to school, which was not very often.

On some days I used to walk down to Main Street where her family operated a storefront fortune telling place. I would wave to her from the street. One day, she told me a poem, which I memorized after asking her to repeat it a couple of times before getting the full impact of the verse. I was so impressed with the poem and so eager to share it with the class that the next day I raised my hand and asked to recite a poem to the class. Mrs. Holt had just assigned us all to read "Requiem" by Robert Louis Stevenson. She didn't mind an interactive classroom environment; as a matter of fact, she encouraged it and invited me up for my recital.

I stood straight and tall and composed, as she had coached us to do. I looked around the room, focused my eyes on the last row and began.

Fifteen minutes of pleasure.
Nine months of pain.
Two weeks in the hospital
And out comes Mary Jane.

As the class broke out in laughter, Mrs. Holt had only three words for me. "Sit down, Stanley!"

Without warning, like a sneak attack in the War we sometimes heard about on the news, I was taken out of the Bond Street Elementary School and out of Asbury Park completely. Pop had arranged with the Jewish Foster Care Agency to relocate me. I was placed in the custody of Dora

Stan Maron

Dorfman, a foster care mother in the Brownsville section of Brooklyn, NY. I do not remember any adverse reaction on my part at the time, maybe because I had been prepped and debriefed by a social worker in Red Bank, New Jersey, who had anticipated that I would be unhappy and protest the change. But I didn't protest, and I didn't act out.

At ten years of age, I was looking forward to the change. It could have been that the social worker did a good job preparing me for the change and I liked her. But more likely it was because I was getting away from my father, who had become more and more distant and morose after my mother's death. He no longer took me to the shop to help with turning collars and other chores. No longer walked home with me after work, sharing small talk and an ice cream cone or a sugar candy.

He was no father to me anymore. It seemed like I was as happy to be rid of him as he was of me.

I was excited about the idea of moving to Brooklyn and was looking forward to leaving Asbury Park. I had visited New York City a couple of times and found it awesome. It reminded me of a big thick magazine with lots of words and pictures that were for real. Everybody walked fast and talked fast and seemed to have important things to do.

I understood that I would only see my father when he came to visit. I don't think that I really got the full impact of what was happening until the rainy Sunday morning that my father and I boarded the train at Penn Station with my small suitcase en route to New York City. I remember thinking that I was going to what seemed like some kind of winter camp.

It all fit together when we arrived at 1983 Strauss Street in the Brownsville section of Brooklyn and were greeted by Mrs. Dorfman and her family. I got involved playing some game with a few of the kids and was kind of surprised when I was told that my father was leaving. I cried a little, but was told that he would come and visit me soon. I do remember right from the start, I had more household chores than I could handle, but I soon got into the swing of things.

Stan

After a breakfast of oatmeal topped with chocolate syrup, Mrs. Dorfman and I walked to PS 175, the community elementary school in Brownsville, Brooklyn. The school wasn't much different from Bond Street School in Asbury Park, except that it was about three times as big and the bricks seemed real old. That kind of intimidated me. I was scared and shy and felt as if I was going to faint. I had certainly changed from the time when my mother had taken me to enroll in first grade at Bond Street School when I went wild and ran all around the school. Now I stood quietly in a disciplined manner, scared shitless as someone examined the records that they had received from Bond Street School. As the person looked at the papers, she began to mumble some stuff which I did not understand at first, but I soon realized her authority when she explained she was the Principal and her name was Mrs. Aldrich.

I began to get her message as soon as she turned to Mrs. Dorfman and asked, "Why in the world would anyone leave a beautiful place like Asbury Park to come to a jungle like Brownsville?" In her inimical style, Mrs. Dorfman just stared her down.

I listened carefully to Mrs. Aldrich's strange welcoming as she had someone usher me to a fifth grade class being taught by a Mrs. Lichtman. At first look I thought Mrs. Licthtman was kind of attractive, but as she began to ask

56

me a bunch of stupid questions about why this and why that and how many brothers and sisters I had, we had already rubbed each other the wrong way. I never even got a chance to tell her about the death of my mother or about my family. Her questions were all stupid.

One of our subjects was geography, which I had very little knowledge of since we did not study much geography in Asbury Park. On one occasion, she asked me what petroleum was and I think I said gas or something.

Mrs. Lichtman marched me into a few other classrooms to put my apparent ignorance on display. On another occasion she found out that I hadn't studied any fractions and was behind the class level in math, so she told me to have my brother the engineer whom I had bragged about to her show me how to do fractions. At that time, my big brother Meyer had a job working as an electrical engineer at the Dumont Television Company in Passaic, New Jersey. He came to visit me on most Sundays. We would talk and sometimes go to see a movie. I looked forward to seeing him and he always liked to hear the off-color jokes I had picked up from the kids in my new household.

I think getting away from Mrs. Lichtman at the end of that first school year in Brooklyn was the happiest day of my school career. Overall, I liked the kids, who were about half Jewish and half black. Mrs. Lichtman was also Jewish, but I think I might have preferred any of the teachers I had in New Jersey to her.

When Meyer came to visit me one Sunday, I told him about the fractions problem. He asked me what kind of fractions she was talking about. When I told him that I didn't even know what fractions were or what she was talking about, he was really puzzled by this. He proceeded to draw a long line with numbers above and numbers below the line. He then showed me how each number could be fit into one on the other side of the line, and that the numbers had proportional qualities that could be broken down into parts. I really didn't understand all of what he was showing me, but must have developed a pretty good conceptual understanding, since I became the best math student in the class and, eventually, probably knew more about fractions than Mrs. Lichtman.

On another Sunday, Meyer and I talked, as usual, about what to do. Meyer suggested that we visit Zaida (Grandpa) Yehuda, our father's father. He said he knew where our grandfather was living at the time and that he would be happy to have a surprise visit from us. I agreed, but explained that I really didn't know Zaida Yehuda. I had only seen him a few times.

I only remember meeting my paternal grandmother once when I was about 3. My father and I visited my Grandma in the Long Branch, New Jersey hospital. She was lying in a bed in a dark room with a few people by her bedside. I remember someone bringing her a glass of orange juice. She drank it without picking her head up from the pillow. She didn't spill a drop on herself. I was amazed and thought that she had done some great feat. A few days later, I was told she had died. I don't remember what my reaction was.

I never got to know those Grandparents at all. I think there was just too much insanity going on between my mother and father to establish any good family relationship.

Meyer told me we could find out all about him if we could locate him. So we set out on the subway for our exploratory visit to Grandpa Yehuda on the Lower East Side of Manhattan. As we rode on the train, I asked Meyer some questions about Grandpa. Meyer said that as a small boy he had visited our Grandpa regularly in Harlem where he was the janitor of a large building. But when our father moved to New Jersey to work with his brother, Meyer didn't see much of our Grandpa and Grandma until they moved to Long Branch, New Jersey, around 1931 to be near their sons. This seemed a little strange to me because it was about family stuff that I was never part of.

Meyer told me that when Grandma died in 1937, Grandpa moved back to the Lower East Side, where he remarried. Meyer visited him and his new bride a few times when he was enrolled in Cooper Union College. I found these details interesting and was looking forward to our get-together with our Grandpa.

When we got off the train, Meyer said he hoped the old guy still lived at the same address. I had been in Manhattan a few time before and now was able to recognize the difference between where I was living in the Brownsville section of Brooklyn and the Lower East Side of New York. It seemed like a different world. The way people dressed, the way they walked, the well-stocked pushcarts with all kinds of produce and soft goods, the traffic, the smell of food cooking in stores, the churches and synagogues all overwhelmed me as we walked. A few times we stopped as Meyer looked around to get his bearings. It wasn't long before we approached a large old tenement with a big lobby and children running in every direction.

After walking up three or four flights, Meyer recognized Grandpa's apartment and knocked on the door. He waited a moment, then knocked even louder. A woman came to the door. She paused a moment. Meyer recognized Grandpa's wife. As he explained who we were, she smiled and said she remembered him. He also said he remembered her name was Rachel. She invited us in and offered us some tea while telling us that Yehuda was at Shull and told us how to get there. We stayed and talked for a few minutes and then explained we would be back a little later.

The Synagogue was only a few minutes' walk from their apartment. Since it was Sunday, there were just a few old guys hanging out and talking in the front of the large prayer room near the altar. The benches were shiny and polished. Meyer mentioned that the floors looked freshly sanded and painted. The place looked spiffy compared to the old unattended synagogue in Asbury Park.

Meyer and Grandpa recognized each other right away. I think Grandpa even recognized me, although I had forgotten what he looked like except for his beard, which I remembered as being long and stringy. As we talked, I began to see the typical Maron look: a ruddy complexion, big round face with a suspicious smile, a prominent nose, and a muscular build, even at his old age of, I think, about 75. He was wearing old worn shoes and a beat up double breasted suit that did have some style.

We went into the garden at the Synagogue and talked. Grandpa Yehuda told us he was the shamus (caretaker) of the Synagogue. Meyer answered a whole lot of questions. Grandpa seemed to know a lot of things about family matters, like what professions and work his sons and grandchildren were doing, who was married and how many children they had. At times during the conversation, he filled in some of the things that Meyer seemed unsure of, which kind of amused me. When he talked about Isadore, the manufacturer, who was his most successful son and who had two sons who were doctors, a son in medical school and two more sons who were doing well in business, his face lit up. At one point, he referred to Meyer as "a big engineer" and said I looked like a very smart boy who would do well in life. Marons aren't always right – sometimes, they are only half right. I think what he was doing was some fact checking just to make sure he had been getting correct information, an old Maron trait.

Although he was in touch with Isadore, he missed my father, who had not seen him in a long time. They had originally come to America together from Russia in 1910. Meyer said our father was very busy in New Jersey. Grandpa made a motion of dealing cards and we all had a big laugh. My father, Grandpa's youngest son, liked to say he was Grandpa's favorite because he had gotten the most beatings back home in Odessa.

As we sat and talked, Grandpa walked over to a closet and took a bottle of wine out. We all, including me, had a drink, and I remember him having a few. Meyer asked our Grandfather questions about his life. Most of the discussion was in Yiddish, but I understood most of it. I had heard the stories from my father about Grandpa Yehuda being a roofing expert in Russia, but didn't mind hearing the stories again, as they were always a little different each time. The constant moving from one town to the next in search of new customers and good dirt to mix for his secret ingredients to seal leaky roofs and the guarantees which he could not always keep kept him and the family moving.

The three of us really laughed and had a good time. After about an hour, we went back to his apartment, which was a long railroad flat with old, well-worn wooden furniture. The lighting was good and the afternoon sun made me feel warm and cozy with my brother and my Grandfather.

Rachel made us some delicious soup and tea and cake as we talked some more. Rachel didn't talk much, but she did show us some pictures of her children and grandchildren. She kept filling our tea glasses all the time. She seemed younger than Yehuda, wore a nice apron, and had long gray hair tied in a bun. I liked Rachel, who was friendly and jovial. I hoped I would have a chance to get to know her better, Brooklyn was not so far from the Lower East Side.

We hugged and shook hands before leaving. Grandpa Yehuda gave me a big kiss. Meyer and I said we would come back to visit again.

On the train ride I was pretty filled in on Grandpa's life, but was curious about his folding bed that I had heard so much about from my brothers. Meyer said he didn't mention the subject at the visit because it was a sensitive issue. As the story went, Grandpa had invented a folding bed in the basement of one of the buildings he was the Super of when he first came to America. He sold the patent to some company and felt he had made a big mistake. The famous "Murphy Bed" became popular all over New York, but Grandpa Yehuda never benefitted from its huge popularity.

Meyer said that Grandpa had tried a few more inventions, but they didn't work out. He soon realized that his son, Isadore, was doing quite well as a garment manufacturer and hit him up regularly for some bucks. Meyer said our father, who seldom saw Grandpa Yehuda, even helped him when he could. I don't think Yehuda was a high liver, but I do remember my father once mentioning that he liked good cigars. That explained the nicotine stains that I saw on his beard earlier in the afternoon.

Yehuda passed away about two years later before we got back for another visit. I did attend the funeral with my father, and when I asked for Rachel, thinking she might have been there, I was told she couldn't come. This made no sense to me. But our family was so crazy, I never knew what the rules were, anyway.

Chapter 7: School Daze

In the Spring my father went to the Hebrew Educational Society to arrange for me to go to Camp Wel-Met for a month in the upcoming summer. Camp Wel-Met, which was located in upstate New York, had a sliding scale, where the payment was determined by the income of the family. My father complained that the price was too high, and that between Mrs. Dorfman and all his expenses he was going broke. It was hard for me to understand this because every time we went out I always noticed his wallet bulging with big bills. I had recently learned the word "bullshit," and I was beginning to recognize it when I heard it. I knew at that time cutters in the ladies coat industry were making about $150 a week, which was good pay.

I liked my counselor at camp because he seemed to take an interest in the kids in our group. Danny played football for Dewitt Clinton High School in the Bronx and liked to talk about his team and his coach. He always asked questions and told us to write cards home to our parents. I wrote a few cards to my father, and he even came up to visit me once. I would have written more to my father, but writing cards cut into my fun time too much. We played all kinds of games. I developed an interest in baseball, swimming and volley ball. At the end of the summer we had a competition, called Capture the Flag, which was a little rough and a lot of fun. It was simply about capturing a flag from the opposing side and running through a goal post. It was similar to rugby. We even had a few dances with girls from another camp, but I was shy at the time and didn't mix much with the girls.

I had a good time and made some fun friends and was sorry when I had to go back to the city at the end of the month.

I liked Mrs. Dorfman, my foster mother, who said I could call her Dora. She was always

Stan and Hymie

clear on what she expected of me and everyone else. She had two sons, who were big guys. I didn't see much of them. The two other kids that she managed, as she liked to describe her job, liked to play board games, which I sometimes played with them. One of the kids was named Solomon. He was a good chess player. We played on a regular basis, though I hardly ever won. When I asked one day about his family, he told me his father went to Canada. I asked whether his father came to visit and his face saddened. I never asked any more about his family, nor did he ask about mine. I tried to tell him a little about Asbury Park and all of my adventures, but he didn't seem interested.

The next school year I entered the 6th and last year of elementary school and had a teacher named Mr. Silver, who I liked. Mr. Silver was a very concerned man who took a special interest in the kids. He always asked questions about my brother Meyer, the engineer, and my brother Hymie, who was in the Air Corps and in aerial gunnery school. I think Mr. Silver knew I was in foster care, but we never got into that. He was big on things like physical culture and nature. Some days he took us across the street from the school to a park where he conducted racing and jumping events, which were called track and field. After these events, we had what he referred to as nature studies, where we learned about plants and flowers.

On May 1, Mr. Silver gave us a short history of working class culture and tradition and taught us a dance done around a maypole. He asked that we dedicate this dance as a ceremony to all the working people of the entire world. Mr. Silver explained that on this holiday we should rejoice in our freedom and the 8-hour work day. I had never heard of this holiday, but agreed the 8-hour day was a good idea and the dance was a lot of fun.

Sometime he would teach what he called "co-education," where the boys and girls danced together after learning a few basic steps. Mr. Silver almost always allowed us to choose our partners. I chose as my dance partner Frances Booth, a beautifully developed black youngster who had recently arrived from South Carolina. As we danced together to some nice music, everything was going along fine until Mr. Silver caught us in the back of the room, where Frances was giving me a lesson in close dancing. We were bonding beyond his expectations. He didn't lose any time in finding us new partners. I think I identified with Frances because she joined our class in the middle of the school year, as I had done the year before. When she arrived in Brooklyn from the South she was not able to read well and was always quiet. It wasn't long before she could read well and was one of the smartest kids in the class.

On one occasion during a glee club recital in the school auditorium, the group was singing a song that went like, "a fish is an animal with long funny ears, it kicks up at everything it hears." Frances became so turned on by this song that she began to sing very loudly while adding some neat choreography. I can still see her singing and dancing with her hair combed straight up long before Don King ever had the idea. I was pissed when the choir leader took her gently by the arm and placed her back in formation. I knew she was a star in the making and complimented her when the class broke for lunch that afternoon. At the end of the school year we had a small graduation ceremony; all the kids signed each other's autograph books with such ditties as, "Take the local, take the express; don't get off 'til you reach success."

The following school year when I was 11, I started Lew Wallace Junior High School. JHS 66 was an all-boys school that lived up to its reputation as a hellhole. What I had heard about the place was, unfortunately, quite accurate. About half of the kids were black and the other half mostly Jewish, similar to the elementary school I had come from. Most of the families of the Jewish kids were first generation immigrants and were either unemployed or working on low paying jobs. Many had recently moved to Brooklyn from the Lower East Side of Manhattan and liked the idea of having more space. As time went on many black families who had recently immigrated from the South in search of better paying jobs arrived and joined the community. JHS 66 was the first school in Brooklyn to have a black principal, Arthur D. Houston. He did make some improvements, but the place was a mess and I am sure very hard for him to manage.

Given the difficult conditions, the kids got along surprisingly well together. When problems occurred they were seldom racial in origin. But looking back, I believe there were some underlying feelings of hostility. By the time that I was entering the 7th grade in 1946, the black and mostly Jewish white kids whose families hadn't left for the Long Island suburbs were about equal in number.

In many cases the racism they encountered in their daily lives was the underlying source of resentment. At times this was quite obvious, although from what I saw these problems were not directly addressed by the teaching staff.

On the first day of our new school year we lined up in "the cage," a fenced-in area outside of the school surrounded by slum buildings, some of which were abandoned. The cage was where we played games like punch ball and stickball during our gym period. It had many purposes. Sometimes, kids would go down to the cage to fight. It's hard to believe now, but on some occasions even a teacher might be spotted in a fistfight with one of the kids. These fights were referred to as rumbles. By the time some of the students reached the 9th grade, their last year, some could be quite menacing and an equal match for any of the teachers. The fights were usually fair, always one on one.

The inside of the building, which was quite old, had a character of its own. The hallways were very long and narrow, and teachers always stood guard during class change. The floors had a thick gray coat of paint and the walls were endowed with a yellow splash of what must have been auto body primer. Each classroom had wooden desks with inkwells that were never used. There was an effort made to plaster the cracked walls, which were painted over with an off-white, chalky substance. The rooms had many windows, some of them always broken. There were two large staircase landings on each of the six floors, and the whole building had an unmistakable odor of damp concrete.

I look back at some of the teachers at this school in disbelief. A few were among the most colorful characters I have ever met and I will never forget them, like the shop teacher, Mr. Tobias, and his assistant, Mr. Lubell. Mr. Lubell was good-natured and never seemed to be bothered by anything, except when the corners of the wood became chipped because of poor planing. He hated wasting wood, since it was rumored that at the end of the term, he and Mr. Tobias took quite a bit of it home for their own projects. Once, a kid in my class had the nerve to mention this to him. Mr. Lubell told the kid that if he were a head bigger, he would take him out to the cage and kick the shit out of him.

Lubell's walrus appearance was pretty threatening. He was average height, but very round like a barrel. His arms were too short for the sleeves on his shirts, so he wore arm bands to shorten the sleeves. When he walked his shoulders sloped and his arms dangled almost touching the floor, even though they were short. He always had a half smile on his face, with his head bobbing from side to side.

The term project consisted of making either a shoeshine box or a small table. I can still hear Mr. Lubell's booming voice hollering, "Straight, smooth and square", meaning straight planing, smooth sanding, and square corners.

I chose to make a shoeshine box, because my friend Leroy told me if I was broke I could make some money shining shoes. One day I took his advice and went down to Pitkin Avenue where the action was and set my box up with some polish and wash and a few rags I had found. I got a couple of customers at a dime each, but after about two hours when it was beginning to get busy on the street, a kid came over and informed me that I was on his spot. I told him that I got here before him and I wasn't going anywhere. He then began handling my shoe polish, opening my few cans which he took out of my box.

Fighting had become a very difficult thing for me to manage, because I never could figure out what to do with my glasses. This time I had put my glasses in the shoe shine box before the incident. I felt I was being bullied and became furious. We both started throwing punches at about the same time and wound up wrestling and punching on the ground. I don't remember who was getting the best of it, but at some point, a cop who was on his beat pulled us apart. Seeming to understand what was happening even before either of us said a word, he told us both to leave and not come back and to go home in different directions, which we did. I walked home thinking I should have made a table, but I did kind of enjoy the early afternoon action.

Mr. Tobias, the main shop teacher, was a dapper little guy about 5'5" who wore neat white shirts and floral pattern neckties under his apron. He affected an Edward G. Robinson style of speaking. He never interacted much with the kids except for the final examination of the term project. He once found a planed edge on a piece of wood that was not straight, smooth and square. He didn't like it and told the kid what was wrong. The kid became defensive and said that Mr. Lubell had found no fault with the work. When Tobias then confronted Lubell, all hell broke loose, with Lubell cursing out both the student for being a snitch and accusing Tobias of not doing a fucking thing all term. Tobias called Lubell a fat prick and said he should keep his fuckin' mouth shut. I don't think anyone really cared what they were arguing about, it was pure entertainment for the class. We all cheered them on, as some hollered "Punch him, kick his ass," thoroughly exasperating both teachers. Things eventually quieted down by themselves and got back to normal.

One day I remember looking out of the window from my home room and seeing Mr. Lubell in a rumble with the toughest kid in the school. Lubell had a flat-footed stance, arms close to his face, chin cocked into his left shoulder for protection, right arm tucked in slightly moving and ready for the release, left arm extended in motion ready to jab. His opponent, David Hunter, a solidly built kid who had a reputation for not only being tough but also being smart, stood about 5' 7" and weighed around 140 pounds, which meant he had about 60 pounds the worst of it. Unlike Lubell, whose style was a dated flat-footed stance, David adapted the contemporary stance of the street: body at a right angle, left arm extended, right arm cocked in front of the face and both arms in constant motion ready for the release while dancing from one side of the opponent to the other, all the time looking for an opening to throw a quick flurry of punches. From what I could see, David used his speed and landed a few good solid shots. Lubell's only opportunity came when he could get in close enough to land a few mostly body punches before David could slide away, doing some neat counter-punching. It ended with Mr. Mirsky, the gym teacher, separating the two, but not before a few solid blows were landed.

As far as I know, neither the teacher nor the student was suspended or punished for the fight. At least, we students never heard about it, and Mr. Lubell was in class the next day, right on schedule.

My homeroom teacher, Mr. Rappaport, was better known as "Rappy the Runt." I don't know who gave him the nickname, but it fit. He was short and emaciated-looking, and when he spoke it was as if he were chirping. He taught typing and was always talking about how students were better years ago. I never took his typing course, but the word was that he didn't teach much of anything. He engaged in an ongoing feud with Miss Tastra, the library teacher. The kids found this rather amusing. I remember Miss Tastra telling us about how "Rappy" was so cheap that when he walked in the street he picked his pant legs up above his knees so as not to lose any vitamin D from the sun. In his turn, Rappy liked to talk about how many husbands Miss Tastra had had.

I did notice that Rappy wore the same suit and worn shoes every day, but I could never figure out why anybody would want to marry Miss Tastra in the first place, even though she did have attractive, steel gray hair.

Mrs. Harrison, one of the two black teachers in the school, taught English. She had a very serious interest in literature and stressed the importance of reading. Her classes were usually interesting, because she mixed her lessons with humor and poked fun at students in a comical way. I remember her calling on Sidney Slavin, whose family was well known in the fish business, to answer a question. The question was how Mark Twain had gotten his pen name. Sidney said he "didn't know because he didn't name him." Mrs. Harrison told him he was excused because he didn't have to know the answer to her question to sell fish, and that even if he did know the answer, it would not get the fish smell out of his clothes. Mrs. Harrison told Sidney that she would excuse the smell as well as him being a dummy if he would please bring her a gefilte fish. I do not know whether he ever brought her anything. Sidney got ribbed for as long as I can remember by kids always asking him, "Have you got Mrs. Harrison's fish today?"

When my friend Leon Kaplan didn't know an answer to one of her questions, she told him that he was getting very fat and that she thought he might be suffering from blubber of the lugger. She did not confine her put-downs to the students in the class. Her favorite targets were her uncles in South Carolina. She loved to talk about how much they thought they knew and how little they really knew. One time she told us a story about how her uncle tried to bake a cake, using sawdust as an ingredient instead of flour.

On one occasion she walked to the window and looked out at where the new housing projects were being built on Osborn Street. She then placed her hands on her hips and declared that she was not going to do a thing until some man who she was watching on the job began to work. One of the kids named Mark Reed pointed out that several workers had already lost their lives on the job she was talking about and that his father was a steel worker and worked very hard. She seemed a little taken aback. Mark gained the respect of the whole class, including Mrs. Harrison, and she did stop bashing the workers.

The Levine brothers taught art and history. One taught higher classes and the other taught the 7th graders. Their classes were quiet and orderly. Sometimes it seemed as if the kids were a bunch of hypnotized mummies. Perhaps there was some mystique in the low deliberate tone of the two teachers' voices when they spoke. The kids were sure afraid of them. I remember that they were both immaculate dressers. I don't remember anything either of them ever taught me, but maybe I learned some discipline from them.

Mr. Conner was a piece of work, cut somehow from the cloth of an 18th century court jester. He taught printing and was good at conveying the development of print media from its inception to the present day. His lessons consisted of picking letters that were in a tray on the end of a thin piece of metal shaped like a toothpick. These letters would be arranged in the desired text. The printer would then ink the letters and impress them on a paper surface to produce the finished product. His more developed lessons consisted of 20th century presses which were run by electricity. We received a pretty good rudimentary understanding of the printing industry. The Board of Ed, as always, seemed unable to afford good modern equipment that would have made things a lot more interesting.

Mr. Conner had one problem that kept him from being a great teacher. He had a short attention span. After about 20 minutes he would become mischievous and begin to implement his ploys. There were many variations, but the general theme always centered on instigating some form of rivalry between two or more students. One of the ploys was to tell a student to keep a watch on the letters in his tray because some student near his workbench was glomming his letters. This would sometimes lead to a fight, in which case Mr. Conner would simply make a hole in the newspaper of his choice, The Journal American, and watch the fight until he or a student decided to break it up.

Miss O.E. Allen, the guidance counselor, was the most feared player in the school. She seemed very old and wore a wig. She had a lot of influence in determining what type of high school a student would go to. When a student reached the 9th grade and was ready for graduation, she had a meeting with the parents and usually tried to sell them on the idea of sending their son to a trade high school. There were many trade schools in the city at that time, such as auto mechanics, aviation skills, textile and needle trades. She pushed hard on this mission because she thought it important to get boys into the trades, especially boys from working class families who would make good union organizers. Her heart was in the labor movement.

Mr. Stiegman, the mechanical drawing teacher, was a little guy who wore the same suit every day and spoke through the side of his mouth like a tough guy. He had a reputation of being a leftist. He always said he liked the class I was in, because the students were down to earth and not snobbish like the kids in the rapid class where the students with high IQs were placed. Occasionally, Mr. Steigman would deliver some kind of a political dissertation. I never really understood what his point was, but he did say demeaning things about the people he called "the capitalists."

One day he gave me a block with a slightly complicated shape and instructed me to draw a top, side and back draft of the block. I worked on this project for a couple of sessions and brought it up to him to be graded. He said it was good and gave me an 'A.' He then pointed to the building being constructed across the street and asked me whether I thought I could design and build a building like that. I said that I didn't think that I could. He insisted that I had the ability, but lacked the tools and went on to explain that the tools were called "capital," which in business terms meant money. I was quite flattered, but continued to reject his argument that the most salient obstruction in my not being able to build such a building was my inability to obtain enough capital. He explained that the capital could buy the people with the knowhow. He gave me something to think about. The few minutes that we talked were one of the more stimulating episodes of my school career. I think he was the first Communist I ever met.

Mr. Epstein, the music teacher, and Mr. Roberts, the social studies teacher, were by far the class act of the school. They had matching personalities, both jovial and warm, and always seemed to have a great time at whatever they were doing. As we entered the room at the beginning of the music period, "Eppy" would be seated at his piano, knocking out some tune like "Give me some men who are stout-hearted men..." or "many long years ago there was a fellow named Robin Hood who used to rob the rich most every chance he could..." The words were written on charts hung from the wall above the blackboard. We all accompanied Mr. Eppy with our adolescent-changing voices. I suspect he thought these songs would be good for character building. Anyway, the class was always an uplifting experience that I looked forward to. Toward the end of the period, we would sing along to "Full Moon and Empty Arms" or maybe "Old Man River."

Mr. Roberts taught history in the room across the hall from Mr. Eppy. Whenever he heard a song he liked, he came into our room and treated us to a solo in his booming voice and dramatic gesturing. I believe he aspired to the opera and took his singing very seriously. So did we, although there was a hint of musical comedy in his stylish delivery. I can still see him standing up in front of the room in his old dapper tan, double-breasted suit, white-on-white shirt, initialed shirt cuffs, and floral patterned necktie, belting out a tune with his self-styled flair and bravado. Often he would talk about the life and accomplishments of a man whom he always referred to as the "great Paul Robeson."

The teacher that I was most impressed with was Mr. Latuer, a black man who had left the South at a young age and traveled to Detroit, Michigan, on his own. He liked to talk about some of his experiences early in his life. He told us that once he was hired as a machinist in an auto plant. Not knowing about the job, he looked at the guy at the next workbench and began to imitate him. After a few minutes, the foreman told him that he could see that he didn't know beans about running a lathe, but since he had a good attitude he would make a good worker and that he would have someone teach him the job. He told us how he enrolled himself in night school and earned a degree in teaching. Mr. Latuer was, for sure, a self-made man.

In the 8th grade I became a problem for everyone around me. My 13th birthday was approaching and it was traditional for a Jewish boy to have a Bar Mitzvah. Mrs. Dorfman had prepared me for this occasion by sending me for the necessary instruction, but I had no interest at all. Religion and its observations were not on my agenda. I began to examine my relationship with my father in a new light. We were in touch, but not seeing each other often. When he did visit there was no warmth in his greeting and there was no sorrow when he left. I had developed hard feelings toward him because I felt he had created my estrangement from my mother's family. Never expressing my feelings about this to anyone, I wished I could have had the support of my grandparents in Asbury Park, but had no way to visit them. For that matter, they never visited me in Brooklyn.

About two months before my 13th birthday in the fall of 1946, a guy started popping up around supper time. He sat and ate with the kids. Mrs. Dorfman introduced him as her friend Aaron and explained he couldn't speak English yet because he had just come to America from Europe a few months before. She said he had been in a concentration camp in Poland during the war.

To my surprise, I found that Aaron did like to talk if someone just spoke his language. When he found out that I knew a little Yiddish from listening to my father and mother before her death, as well as hearing my grandparents talk when I visited them in Asbury Park, he opened up to me. I was the only kid at the house able to communicate with him.

At first I had a hard time understanding most of what he said because he spoke with an Eastern European-inflected accent as opposed to a more American-style Yiddish, where many American words were mixed in. But I really found meeting Aaron interesting. Here was a guy like someone out of a movie telling me about things I had only heard second-hand or in the newsreels. He never talked much about himself, but did tell me he worked in a warehouse in Manhattan. I was surprised because he always wore a nice cool suit, but I guess he just liked to dress up. Our conversations skipped around a lot and he would change subjects when I asked questions about things he did not want to get into. As time went on, I found out that Mrs Dorfman had met him on Sunday afternoon at folk dancing at the Hebrew Education Society on Hopkinson Avenue. This information was given to me by Mrs. Dorfman's sister, who came to cover for Dora on Sunday afternoons, and it filled my curiosity about where Mrs. Dorfman had met Aaron.

One discussion that we often had and about the only thing that Aaron stressed was the importance of a Jewish Homeland and the importance of Jewish Nationalism. When he found out that I wasn't interested in having a Bar Mitzvah he became angry and showed dissatisfaction in my attitude. As the day of my 13th birthday approached, my father, Mrs. Dorfman and Aaron pressured me into having a small ceremony. I chose the place, an old, beat up synagogue in the neighborhood. My Hebrew school education back in Asbury Park with Mr. Reisman came in handy. A local Rabbi agreed to walk me through a few prayers, which I was told I recited well, and the show was a hit.

My father's brother, Isadore, and his three sons, my father and my brothers, Meyer and Hymie and Mrs. Dorfman and her boyfriend Aaron were about the only ones who attended. I could have invited my Grandfather and my mother's sister and I think they would have attended, but the pain and bad feelings between my father and my mother's family and my sense of embarrassment were more than I could handle. I hoped they understood.

No provisions had been made for a traditional party celebration after the ceremony. Isadore, my father's older brother, was still grieving for the loss of his wife, my Aunt Sadie, who had recently passed away. Explaining that people had driven from New Jersey and were hungry, Isadore offered to take us all out to eat in one of the restaurants in the area. Jake agreed and recommended the Little Oriental, an upscale kosher restaurant. He said it was his party and he would pay and did apologize for the whole poorly planned event. A little argument took place. Finally the two old guys who had been through so much settled on splitting the check. I liked that idea because, after all, it was our party as my father had said. And besides, I felt I was the one who screwed it up in the first place. I enjoyed seeing my father and his brother interact; it gave me a feeling of family - something I had been missing for a long time.

Isadore was one of the early developers of the garment assembly line in the mid-1920s. He always prided himself on running an open air shop with windows on all sides. Unlike my father, he was not a union supporter, but he did not fight against union organization.

My father had not been on good terms with Isadore. Like many of the people in my father's life, he had a somewhat turbulent relationship with his brother. There was also a matter never discussed, at least in my presence: When Isadore had built the factory in Asbury Park many years ago, my father moved from New York to work there. As I remember Isadore, he was a tough, hard-working man who paved his road to success the hard way and had high expectations of others. Maybe he wanted more of

Jake than was possible for his brother to give. I really don't know what had transpired between them, but I did often hear my father say nasty things about Isadore.

Sometime around 1938 Isadore sold the factory and went into business in New York. He kept his shop there and continued to live in Asbury Park up to his last years. My father continued to work for the people who bought the shop in Asbury Park.

I did stay for a short time in the home of Isadore and his family in Asbury Park after the death of my mother. He and his wife made things pleasant for me during a difficult time in my life. Although my father did not get along with Isadore, he had great respect for him. Whenever he told me anything about Isadore he always referred to Isadore by saying, "nobody was smarter than Izzy".

I was given a few cash presents and a nice fountain pen as Bar Mitzvah gifts. It turned out to be a pretty good day.

Chapter 8: Lure of the Street

Around this time, Mrs. Dorfman began complaining about me not getting along with her other foster child, whose name was Melvin. She also said that I was not obeying her and that I was staying out too late at night. I did stay out at the community center, where I liked to play ping pong, but she never really told me to come home earlier. And as for Melvin, I couldn't understand what she was talking about since I never even spoke with him. I think she thought I was being disrespectful to her and I probably was. I was becoming difficult and was not satisfied with any aspect of my life. She told me that she had complained to the agency and that they were going to get in touch with my father.

Meyer was still working as an engineer in New Jersey; Hymie was now out of the Air Corps and in his senior year studying engineering at Rutgers University in New Jersey. They both visited me on an occasional basis. My father had been getting reports, since he was actually paying for most of my upkeep, and he also visited me from time to time. Also, my father and I did speak at my Bar Mitzvah party. He said now that I was growing up, maybe he would move to New York where he could work and be near me. I was not excited about the idea, and when I showed my dislike for the proposal he dropped it, at least for the time being.

The summer before I entered the 9th and final year of Junior High School, I received a letter from my Aunt Blanche and Uncle Max inviting me to spend the summer with them in Sea Bright, New Jersey. As Aunt Blanche put it, I could stay and "just keep an eye on our son, Leonard." Leonard was four years younger than me. I had gotten to know him a little when I was living in New Jersey.

I always liked my Aunt Blanche and had fond memories of rubbing knees with her in my Grandma's house as she taught me to play the Ouiji board. The prospect of getting out of the city seemed pretty good to me and made me feel a lot better. I went as soon as school ended.

At first, I took Leonard to the beach every day, except when it rained. On rainy days, when I thought I could just take it easy, I was asked to help out in their store, which was a block from the beach. After a while I got to like working in the store more than going to the beach. This presented a problem, since when I was working there was no one to watch Leonard.

I liked hanging around with my Uncle Max and talking with him when we had time. I met some of his cronies, the other businessmen in town, like Mickey Sweeney, who ran an appliance store and always told Uncle Max about the wonderful new appliances that would help Max in his business, and Harry, who had started out as a fisherman and then opened his own seafood restaurant. I once overheard some guy joking about Harry being a Sea Bright clam digger in his youth and I will never forget Harry's comeback. He shot back, "It doesn't matter where you come from - it's where you're going that counts." Harry's seafood restaurant was one of the most successful businesses on the Jersey Shore.

I learned more about Max and how he got to Sea Bright, New Jersey. The building was empty when Uncle Max first took it over. At first, he used the space to rent sections to various people who needed storage. Once I asked him who all the people were who rented the space and why they needed storage space. He said, "I don't care as long as they pay the rent."

With his first shop, he sold only a few items, like hot dogs, cigarettes and soda. After about a year, he added a food counter and started to sell some of my aunt Blanche's home cooked delights. Their supper specials were interesting combinations, like borscht and chicken cacciatore, followed by espresso and anisette and maybe a piece of strudel. I loved her corned beef and cabbage.

As time went on, Max and his partner Ding started running a crap game after midnight attended by the local fishermen and some of the other townspeople. Ding had a nice house overlooking the ocean. Leonard and I used to go for a walk to see him sometimes. His wife Gina always gave us soda and cake or a sandwich. On one visit, my curiosity came out and I asked Ding what kind of work he did before what he called his retirement. The answer was clear and simple. "You don't wanna know, Kid."

I never asked him any more questions.

It was hard to figure out when my uncle slept. In a discussion between Max and one of his buddies I heard Max say he was renting space to a couple of local contractors and construction guys to store paint and other materials that they had stolen or purchased on the black market. Max, "the little Jew from Newark", as his buddies and only his buddies called him, knew how to make a buck.

He was good-natured and could take a little ribbing, but on one occasion, a guy crossed the line by speaking rudely to my Aunt Blanche. Max walked around the counter and asked him to leave the store. The guy refused, became boisterous and pushed Max. That was a big mistake. Max threw a volley of punches that floored the guy. The police, ambulance, and fire department were all called, but the guy seemed ok and just left, as they say, the hard way. No charges were ever made against my uncle.

The police and fire captains were both his drinking buddies.

When I got back to Brooklyn at summer's end, nothing had gotten better. My Aunt Blanche had mentioned once during the summer that maybe I should stay on with them. That probably would have been a good idea, but I didn't take her up on it because sometimes Max was a very hard guy for me to get along with. I liked him, but he wanted me to work almost all of the time. I also did not find Sea Bright to be an interesting place to live, especially during the winter months. Looking back, I think I should have given it a chance.

At around this time I became depressed and didn't know what was happening with me. When my brother Hymie, whom I hadn't seen for some time, visited during his Christmas vacation from college, he made a great effort to tutor me in algebra, but I was unable to concentrate on what he was showing me and began to feel bad. It was only my adolescent pride that kept me from crying. Hymie felt bad, too. Mrs. Dorfman suggested that I get some kind of therapy, but neither my father nor my brother took the idea seriously, and it never happened.

One of my favorite pastimes was visiting luncheonettes, hangouts for guys of all ages, usually located in my neighborhood. I really wasn't old enough to hang out with these guys and didn't fit in, but I did find their conversations interesting. It was one of my favorite forms of entertainment, and I began coming home later and later. Mrs. Dorfman was losing patience with me. On one occasion she said she was going to get in touch with my father.

I don't know what transpired between my father and

the foster care agency, but it wasn't long before my father found a furnished room a few streets from where I had been staying and moved from Asbury Park to Brooklyn. I visited him on occasion at his place. We decided that when another room became available in the house I would move in. Soon after, a room opened up and he made the necessary arrangements. Pop decided that I would continue to eat suppers at Mrs. Dorfman's. My father gave me money to buy breakfast and lunch in one of the luncheonettes in the neighborhood. I found this arrangement enjoyable and was beginning to feel very grown up at the age of 13.

When I received my report card at the end of 9th grade, I had failed every subject. My father and I were scheduled to meet with Miss Allen, the guidance counselor, to discuss my high school placement. She explained that I needed to pass at least two subjects to graduate from junior high school and get into high school. She said this could be done in summer school, I could go on to Brooklyn Automotive High School in the fall, or I could be left back to repeat the 9th grade. Although I was against the idea of going to a trade school, my father became partly sold after hearing her argument about the importance of getting smart working class boys from union backgrounds into the trades so they could improve conditions for the working class. My father was always a soft touch for a pro-union argument, but I objected strongly. I said I wanted to go to an academic high school.

This was an introductory lesson in cutting a deal. I chose summer school at Erasmus Hall, where I repeated English and Social studies. I passed, and it wasn't bad at all. There were even girls in the classes, a new experience, since my junior high had been all boys. The teacher was a nice woman and I liked every class.

That fall, I started at S.J. Tilden High School. The classes were large. I was in the late session, which meant that my first class was at one o'clock, giving me plenty of time to sleep. It didn't take long before I realized that the classes were above my head, and so were the girls I was interested in. Extreme shyness and thick eyeglasses made me feel uncomfortable in the company of the opposite sex and kept me from dating. After receiving my second report card that was not impressive, I was given a note requesting my presence at the guidance counselor's office. The counselor switched me to a commercial course, where I studied merchandising, typing and bookkeeping. With the exception of the merchandising course, my interest in school was gone.

In my second year at the school, one of the gym teachers suggested that I try out for the football team. I soon found out that my reflexes were slow because of my poor eyesight, which did not help my depression. I was unable to read the plays fast enough to be a defensive guard. I dropped out of school unofficially, since the law required that a student be 16 to be signed out by a parent. I was only 15, but nobody seemed to miss me. My father knew that I wasn't going to school, but he didn't say much. I think he was disappointed and sad that I was so out of control.

I think being left to my own devices worked best for me. I played a little ball, became interested in weightlifting and joined a gym. I did feel better with a regular place to go and people to talk to.

One day, a discussion with a guy a little older than me turned into an altercation. The argument had something to do with a sports bet we had made. We both felt we had won by the point margin. We were standing in front of the corner luncheonette on Amboy Street when the discussion turned into a pushing match. In a split second, he removed a long metal pole from a hook. The pole was used to turn the awning. He raised it and was getting ready to hit me. He had just made his school's baseball team, and that success may have gone to his head.

He was one of the local bullies I had been afraid of for a long time. This time was a little different and a surprise for him. I grabbed the metal awning turner, which was about four feet long with a built in hand grip for turning. I pushed him in the direction of the window, which I did not mean to do. Luckily, even though the window shattered and he wound up lying on a pile of broken glass, only his arm was cut, requiring some stitches. When it healed in about two weeks he was able to return to baseball practice. He never had much to say to me after that, though he did look at me in a nasty way, as if I had treated him unfairly.

I made friends with some of the guys who worked out in the gym, and I got along pretty well with them. Walter Bookbinder, one of the guys who was a little older than me, went on to become a professional wrestler. He always invited me to go to his matches to keep him company and cheer for him. Walter was a creative person whom I really admired. He became a merchant seaman when he was only 14 years old by falsifying his age. We always had much to talk about. We hung out together and drank a lot of beer, which he swore was a healthy drink. Sometimes we would go up to Abe Goldberg's Gym on the Lower East Side and get in a workout.

Two years into our friendship, Walter began to tell me that he thought he could do better on the West Coast. He moved out to California and established himself under the name of Ray Stern. He invited me to visit him, but I didn't feel I would fit in, so I never went.

I also hung out with a guy named Marvin Dick, who became a mid-level lightweight boxer in the 1950's. Sometimes, I would go to the gym with him when he went to work out. The Biltmore Gym was in the back section of a large pool hall on Livonia Avenue in the East New York section of Brooklyn. I played pool when I got tired of watching boxers punch heavy bags and spar with each other. The guys who trained in this gym were mostly Jewish. Many were main event fighters at the old Madison Square Garden, like Herby Katz, Harold Green, Georgie Small, and Herby Kronowitz.

When I hung out in the gym, it never failed that some guy, a trainer or a manager, would come up and ask, "You wanna' box, kid?" I always shook my head "no." I would have liked to box, but knew my poor eyesight was too much of a handicap.

A few times I did put the gloves and headgear on and went a round or so with Marvin. It didn't take long for me to find out that if a guy is not well trained, a three-minute round can feel like a lifetime, or even end a life. Boxers are respected for the sharp moves they make in the ring. Being able to take punishment is a big part of what makes a boxer good. Jake La Motta, the famous middle weight, built a reputation on never having been knocked off his feet. The sport was not for me; I was smart enough to know that much.

I liked hanging out around Amboy Street, one of the most active streets in the Brownsville section of Brooklyn. On weekends there were always dice games on each corner. The characters playing dice were very colorful. My instinct told me that I wasn't going to get anywhere in school, so I figured I might as well do something where I could make some money. One of the guys told me about his uncle, who owned a small company, the Andrea Sweets Corporation. What his Uncle Mike did was purchase large barrels of little peanut butter candies and put them into one-pound boxes. He sold them to stores, plus he had kids peddle the candies. I started to sell candy for him.

The method I used was to go to busy shopping streets like Broadway in Brooklyn or Pitkin Avenue and give a sample out of a freshly opened box with a nice clean plastic spoon. The candies were sweet and had a pretty good taste, especially when a store worker or consumer was hungry in mid-afternoon. After giving out a sample to 10 or 15 people, I would ask if anyone wanted to purchase a box for just a special advertising offer of only 99 cents. I got 50 cents on each box I sold. On a good Friday or Saturday I could sell as many as 20 boxes, which wasn't a bad afternoon's pay in those days.

Most times, I bought clothes with my earnings and frequented the dice games. The only guys who seemed to win consistently were the guys who were known as hustlers, or wrong betters. These characters would always bet against the roller who shot the dice. They would win by betting even money (the odds were supposed to be 6 to 5) against 8s and 6s, whenever those points came up or whenever someone wanted to bet that an 8 or 6 would come before a 7. The average person did not understand the advantage of such a small edge, but the hustlers, who were for the most part disliked, did. They were usually older and almost always started the games by just going up to a bunch of guys who were hanging out on a corner and throwing a pair of dice on the ground against a wall.

On the weekends there were games on almost every hangout corner in Brownsville. Those who participated were mostly poor working class guys. Some of the more social minded citizens would call the police as a result of the loud talk and bad language. When the police, referred to as "Bulls", would approach in old cars, everyone would run like hell, leaving some money on the ground, which the police were sure to pick up.

This usually amounted to a couple of bucks, which added up nicely for the Bulls on a busy Saturday afternoon, with so many games going in the neighborhood. At other times, they would do a two-car panzer, or approach by foot, trapping the players in the middle before it was possible to run. This led to an arrest, a "pinch." All the players were taken to night court and had to pay a small fine. The Bulls actually preferred the former approach of just grabbing as much money as they could. A pinch was usually made when the precinct captain got "heat" from downtown where the big brass and police commissioner's offices were located. Pinches were then ordered against small offenders in order to cover up some of the more sophisticated gambling operations in the area run by bookies, who paid big bucks to stay in business and were well protected by the powers that be.

One famous case was the Harry Gross case, which ended in 1951 with Gross being busted after years of conducting his bookmaking operation. His income was assessed by the media at $50 million a year, which was bullshit, but a patsy was needed. He fit the bill, mainly because he made himself obvious by wearing flashy clothes and living a high profile life.

Even though I was making some money and sometimes won at pool or dice, I was usually broke. Occasionally I would borrow a buck or two to carry me over until the next day. I usually went to restaurants around Saratoga and Livonia Avenues, hangouts for all kinds of marginal characters. A few years earlier, around 1940, this corner had been a place where the gang called Murder, Inc. had their meetings. This was documented by the District Attorney Burton Turkis, who wrote a book titled Murder Incorporated based on the actual facts of his prosecuting several of these actors, Abe Rellis and Gurah Shapiro, just to name two.

Now the corner had become a popular meeting place for heroin addicts, gamblers and marginal type characters. Once the addicts had scored their drug, "smack" or "shmeck," and had a sufficient high, they loved nothing more than to talk, listen to music and nod off. One of them, a guy called Fourteen, could do a caricature of anybody he ever knew. He was one of the funniest people I have ever known. One day I asked him why they called him Fourteen. He told me that it was short for "Seven and Seven." Fourteen was a member of the Greenberg family. His father and brothers were doing well in the scrap metal business at the time. He liked to tell stories about how his father and brothers were slaving away in the family business while he was just laying back and enjoying his high. Actually, they were supporting his habit and were constantly trying to rehabilitate him, but it never seemed to work. From knowing Fourteen, I realized that, when I had kids of my own, I would never give large allowances, they would just use it for liquor and drugs.

Another of the local shmeckers was Harvey, who had a great interest in cool jazz and wanted to play the saxophone professionally. It may have been his drug habit that got in the way, but he never realized his ambition. He did, however, meet and fall in love with a drop dead beautiful woman named Jessica, who happened to be black. At first his relationship with Jessica was hard for his mother, an old world Russian Jewish woman, to understand and get comfortable with. It wasn't long before he married Jessica. In a short time it became an everyday occasion to see Jessica and his mother walking and talking and hanging out together on a regular basis. Harvey also had two kids with Jessica and stayed away from drugs.

Another one of the addicts was a guy about 25 years old, Little Butch. Because Little Butch had a bad stuttering problem, it was hard to follow what he was trying to say. But everyone who heard him stutter always nodded in approval in a respectful way. Several of these guys wound up going to a federal drug rehab facility in Lexington, Kentucky, one of the first of such places to be established in the United States

Then there was Philly (Nightlife), a frustrated stand-up comedian. Philly had very long hair and was always talking about going to the barber to get an estimate for a haircut. He smoked long cigars and joked about buying them by the foot. He also said he was going to learn a trade so that he would know what kind of work he was out of. Whenever a police car drove past the corner with their sirens on he would declare, "Another cop goin' to lunch." He said he would get married, but he couldn't see himself supporting a strange woman.

There was another guy called Lefty who put people down in a good natured way and was also funny. He dressed in a neat sport jacket and pointed with his index finger while he shuffled on his feet. He reminded me of the way boxers moved.

Lefty liked to talk about people who either knew or thought they knew everything. He referred to these guys as "actors" and said they could make a great argument for when some baseball manager should have taken the pitcher out, or intentionally walked a batter or put a pinch hitter in or called for the batter to bunt or steal a base and all kinds of other stuff they thought they knew all the answers to, but couldn't figure out that if they formed a union and negotiated a contract with their bosses it would improve their living conditions.

One day I saw him talking to a bunch of horse players

who always came to the corner to get a car pool together to go out to Belmont or Aqueduct race tracks where the turf races took place, or Roosevelt Raceway where the trotter horses who pulled carriages raced. He even complimented these guys by telling them he was amazed at how much they knew about horses, like the horse's age, his total record for speed in all kinds of different weather conditions, and how many long or short races the horse won in his last ten races.

He always kidded these guys about why such smart guys couldn't figure out the importance of forming unions. The guys seemed to like him and seemed interested in what he had to say when he came to the corner. One time I remember one of the guys asking Lefty, how do you know who belongs to a union and who doesn't, what are you the FBI? We all laughed, including Lefty.

When my father got home from work, he would look for me on the corner and ask if I had eaten. When I was hungry, I could always count on him for a couple of bucks, but as time passed I refused his money out of shear pride. He would try to talk to me. He said I was ruining my life, and that my brothers, Meyer and Hymie, never did these things. Ironically, he could not offer himself as a role model. He usually played cards and drank in one of the neighborhood storefront social clubs with his buddies until late hours. Those men played mostly sociable pinochle or poker for small stakes, but on the weekends some heavy gambling took place. Pop also liked the racetrack, which he attended on most Saturdays. He claimed not to be a big bettor, but he loved the action and excitement. I believe he was covering up and was in denial about his gambling habit, which he hung onto until his last years of retirement in Florida.

In Brownsville, many of the kids gravitated to the poolrooms once they outgrew playing schoolyard softball and street games. The pool and billiard tables were used as a front for sports betting, the real business, which was illegal. The admission age to the poolroom was sixteen, but I started going there about six months before my 16th birthday. My father wasn't very happy with my newfound hangout. He said nice people didn't go to poolrooms. I really did wonder who the hell he thought I was.

Whatever anyone said about the poolroom didn't make much of a difference to me. The place became my home. I knew that the poolroom was the center of the local gambling operation, where Ben and Jack, the two brothers who owned the place, made book. There was a back room equipped with a ticker tape with all the games and betting odds for every college and professional sporting event. The ticker tapes were read by the houseman and transcribed on a big blackboard placed in the common area for everyone to see. Sometimes games would be taken off the betting board when there was reasonable suspicion about a game.

The year was 1950. Many of the college games were being fixed by professional gamblers who paid the players a pittance to manage the final outcome of the game. This was called point shaving. A team could win a game, but not by the amount of points that they were favored to win by. A bettor who had placed a bet on the losing team would collect winnings even though his team had lost the game. Sometimes a team would even lose the whole game intentionally.

The kingpin of this gambling scheme was a sharpshooter wise guy named Edward Salazo, who claimed to have been in the jewelry business. He enlisted several great young athletes by promising large sums of money. Once the fixing scheme was exposed and arrests were made, several promising athletic careers were destroyed. Solazzo and a couple of the athletes served short jail sentences.

Chapter 9: No More Teachers, No More Books

As soon as I turned sixteen, my father and I made a trip to Tilden High School. He had gotten a letter in the mail that had recorded my truancy and threatened some form of legal procedures if we did not come and straighten out my attendance record. Actually, this turned out to be a ploy to get my father to come in so that he could sign me out of the school. I had almost forgotten where the place was. When he signed the necessary papers for my termination, I felt both anger and shame. When I looked into my father's face, I saw a wounded man. I said that I would try night school but never did, since I was having too much fun at the time and did not want my schedule interrupted.

It was about noon when we finished at Tilden. My father said he had to go back to work. His parting words that day were, "Now that you're not in school, you hef to get a job." My father's work ethic was second to none. After all, wasn't he the guy who left me alone when I was sick in the house on Monroe Avenue in Asbury Park because he had to go to work?

My job hunt did not go well. I went to a few job placement agencies, but had little success. On one occasion, a prominent Wall Street firm where I had applied to work in the mailroom told me that they had a quota for hiring Jews and they would call me later. Growing more and more frustrated, I finally asked my father if he could get me a job. He replied that he had always wanted his sons to be more than tailors, but he would try. Meanwhile, I continued to hang around the poolroom. Although I was becoming less abrasive, I still got into altercations.

One night, my father told me that he had spoken to an old friend in the union hall about getting me a job. The man was now a business agent for ILGWU Local 10, the garment cutters union. He gave my father the name of a man for me to see, the shop foreman. I was hired to work in the shipping department of a factory located on 37th Street and 8th Avenue in the heart of the garment center. My job was to pack coats into large boxes and at the end of the day bring them to the parcel post truck for shipment all over the country. I also made deliveries to many warehouses with a hand truck, which was nothing more than a long slab of wood with bars attached to hang coats on, and a bar to push or pull, depending on whether there were one or two "boys" assigned to doing the delivery.

Sometimes I would stop and play a number with Benny, a bookie on the corner of 38th Street and 8th Avenue. Everybody said he was good and always paid promptly when someone hit. My number was 369 because I remembered that when I was a small boy I once told my mother that I had dreamt about a ring. Being a small stakes numbers player herself, she looked up the number for a ring in a dream book and it showed 369. I do not consider myself a gambler anymore, but this has become my lifelong lucky number. I never won anything with the digit, as numbers were referred to, but maybe it made me feel some kind of bond with my mother, who I wish I had gotten to know better.

I found the city streets interesting and liked getting out of the shop. After a while, I found the inside work boring. Sometimes the cutter asked me to help him spread goods on the cutting table. This was a process I had seen done as a child in Asbury Park, but I wasn't a good candidate for learning the cutting trade. What made the job tolerable was the showroom model, Vivian. She was beautiful and talked funny, always telling us stories about growing up in Kansas. The word was that she was built like a "brick shit house." I wasn't much of an authority on the subject, since at age 17, I hadn't ever been inside of a brick shit house or a model, but I was sure which I would have preferred. When she walked by my packing table she would sometimes pinch me. I looked forward to this as one of the high points of the job. She even told me I could pinch her back and I wish I had. I was still really bashful.

The head shipping clerk, a guy named Harold, who claimed to be the best handball player in the city, told me that Vivian also used to go out with some of the buyers in order to secure big orders for the boss. One time I overheard an argument where the boss called her a whore and she called him a pimp.

When the season ended and business slowed down, I was laid off, as was traditional in the industry. I went to the local unemployment office and registered for a weekly check. I was now a full-fledged member of the working class. I soon found that some of the poolroom regulars considered unemployment a paid vacation, and knew many tricks for how to avert having their checks cut off as a penalty for not searching for work. I really wanted to do more than just hang out. I had become bored with this lifestyle. Nothing seemed to be happening that really interested me.

My father and I shared a room and kitchen privileges in various boarding houses, but we always ate in restaurants. I grew to like vegetables; a vegetable plate was $.90 for three vegetables.

The landlady's son at one place we lived in was an engineering student. He told me that during his summer vacation from college, he worked in the Catskill Mountains as a waiter and explained where I could get a job. Saying they preferred experienced workers, he gave me the names of a couple of places I could say I had worked at and use as references. He said since it was now the off-season, it wouldn't be easy for me to get hired. He suggested that I go for a job as a busboy and just watch how the waiter works. According to him, during the summer season it would be easy to get a waiter's job.

The next morning I went to Anne Jupitor, the placement agency he had suggested on 62nd Street and Lexington Avenue. It was in a big loft on the third floor of a brownstone building. The first thing I saw were men seated at desks behind a wood railing and a group of mostly men conversing in a large waiting area while smoking cigarettes or chomping on big cigars. A man who was standing in the front of the room asked me what kind of work I did. When I answered that I was a busboy, he told me to take a seat and that I would be called shortly.

Curious about the conversations going on around me, I listened in. Most of the talk was about working conditions in the different hotels for cooks or waiters. Some of the cooks boasted about large salaries they had made in past seasons, and the waiters talked about which hotels were good tipping houses and which were bad. I was beginning to feel shy and fearful. My first inclination was to leave the place and head back to the poolroom, but my stronger instincts took over.

After a while, one of the men seated behind the railing called my name and motioned for me to come to his desk. When I sat down he asked me where I had worked in the past. I mentioned the name of the place I had memorized as my place of reference and said that I had worked there last summer. He seemed impressed and began to tell me about how the Catskills were growing and becoming a year round resort. He had a job at the Concord Hotel for a busboy. He said I could make good tips and advised me to take the job. He instructed me on what bus to take, and who to ask for when I arrived. He told me that there was a $2 fee for the job and that I should be at the hotel by 11:00 the next morning. I thanked him and left, happy to have a job and a place to live.

It seemed my life was finally coming together.

Chapter 10: At The Concord

The night I told my father about my plan to work as a busboy in the Catskills he didn't comment much. I don't think he liked the idea, but he knew I wasn't asking his advice. He did say that it might be good for me to get away and asked me to write him, which I never did.

A combination of fear and anxiety kept me from sleeping that night. I knew I had to make some changes in my life, but didn't know if becoming a busboy was a good choice. I hadn't been feeling good about how things were going and saw this as a chance to rearrange my young life.

After a sleepless night, I followed the directions that were given to me by the man at the agency and arrived at the bus line to Monticello, New York, in time for the first bus out. When I called the hotel as I had been instructed, the man who answered the phone asked me some questions. When he found out that I was a new dining room employee asking for a ride to the hotel, he told me that he didn't have a driver and hung up the phone. At this point I was mad. I wasn't about to be discouraged by some jerk who I was already planning to get even with. After all, didn't the man at the employment agency tell me to just call when I got to the bus station and I would be picked up? I called the hotel again, this time telling the person on the other end that I had just been hung up on and needed a ride. This guy was a little more understanding and told me that he would try to get someone there to pick me up before noon. But I was too impatient to wait.

When I was small, my brother Julius would sometimes

tell me about his hitchhiking experiences. I decided to try. I asked the ticket clerk in the station which direction the Concord was and he pointed the way. I went out to the street, put my thumb out as Julius had showed me and, in a short time, a woman in a station wagon stopped and asked where I was going. When I said the Concord Hotel, she told me to throw my bag in the back and jump in. She asked me about myself. I told her that I was sent by an agency to work as a busboy at the hotel. She told me that she was a waitress in the main dining room and that she would take me to Irving, the headwaiter, when we arrived at the Concord. She seemed a bit surprised to hear that I was from New York City, since at that time most of the workers at the hotel were from Pennsylvania. She introduced herself as Bobbie and was a talkative person. Bobbie was a short woman with a muscular, yet shapely and quite feminine figure. She offered me a cigarette, but I didn't feel like smoking. She lit one for herself. Bobbie told me about all the layoffs that were taking place in the coal mining and steel industries in Pennsylvania and how people were now coming to resorts in the Catskills to take whatever work they could get to make a living.

I was enjoying our talk and felt more comfortable than I had in the past when speaking with a young lady. After parking her car in the staff parking area, Bobbie and I went into the dining room, which looked like a neat place to me. I'd never seen anything like it except in movies; so many large tables with neat white table cloths, all set up with shiny silver utensils, lots of windows and flowers all over the place.

She pointed to Irving, the headwaiter. I thanked her and said good bye. At that time, the Concord was the premiere hotel of the entire area and had only one rival, Grossingers, which was a bit more established and catered to a more conservative crowd. However, the Concord enjoyed the reputation of being able to provide a fun time for a hipper, action-seeking vacationer, maybe even romance for a single person seeking a relationship.

As I approached the entrance to the dining room, Irving stood in front of a podium covered with some papers which I later learned were his seating plans. I handed him my contract from the employment agency. He took a quick glance at it and proceeded to look me over from head to foot, the likes of which I had never experienced in my young lifetime. The look was followed by a vocal roar which seemed to make the walls shake. "Where the fuck have you been until 11:30 in the morning?" he said. "You were supposed to be here to work breakfast."

As I started to explain my transportation problem, he motioned to a guy who was standing nearby, instructing him to take this "cock-eyed fuck" to the housekeeper to get a room and have him back to work lunch in 45 minutes. For some unknown reason I did not feel abused. Later I learned that this was Irving's brand of Catskill mountain humor. It matched the kind of humor I had heard in Brooklyn.

The guy he assigned to take me to the housekeeper introduced himself as Seymour. Seymour talked non-stop. He was an encyclopedia on the Catskill Mountains resort hotel industry and I hung on every word he said. After throwing my suitcase on a cot in the room which I was to share with three other busboys, Seymour hustled me back to the dining room to work lunch. Little did he or Irving know that I knew as much about bussing tables as I did about flying a helicopter. Seymour brought me to Scottie, a man who he referred to as a captain, and left. Scottie had the accent to match his name. He asked me several questions about my past experience as a busboy. Some of them were a bit tricky, like, "Who was the headwaiter at the..." whatever hotel I was claiming to have worked at in order to fake my experience. As our conversation progressed, I began to see the look in his face change from merely being puzzled to one of disbelief, and finally sheer amazement. Some of the questions he asked were kind of vague and when I tried to fill in the spaces by making up information, like a made-up name of the headwaiter, Scottie knew I was making stuff up. After a few minutes of interrogation, he looked squarely into my face and asked, "Do I look like a fuckin' moron to you?"

I answered loud and clear, "No!" We smiled at each other and he assigned me to a waiter who he said would have time to "break me in." The guy's name was Donnie. He was from the Bronx. Donnie was a skinny, fastidious sort of guy with what might be called shifty eyes. His first question to me was where I had put my shovel. I told him that I did not have a shovel. He insisted that all of the new employees coming from everywhere have shovels and pickaxes. This was his brand of bigoted humor, spiced with a bit of Bronx sarcasm, shedding light on the new rivalry between the old time Jewish mountain waiter, usually a gambling, fast buck type, and the new out-of-work Polish-American coal miner from Scranton or one of its nearby towns. He told me that the Pennsylvania waiters get all the good tipping guests because they want to have a union and the bosses were scared of them and wanted to buy them off, and "we get shit."

As the guests began coming in for lunch, Donnie pointed out the three tables we were covering and explained that I was in charge of serving beverages such as coffee, tea, and, of course, water. He showed me how to pick up the dirty dishes and how to stack and carry the full tray to the kitchen dishwashing area. After working a couple of meals and taking Donnie's sharp instruction liberally laced with criticism, I felt like a pro who had made the big leagues. My fortune awaited me.

The first group of guests we served were women conventioneers from the B'nai Brith organization. They were friendly folks and asked me questions, like was I a college student and where was my home? I think their interest was well-intentioned, but their expectations of who I was were a bit misplaced. The convention ended Sunday after we served lunch. We cleaned up and set our tables for our next batch of guests who were scheduled to arrive for dinner.

After setting up, we were called to the headwaiters area where we were given a blanket tip by the assistant to the headwaiter, a man who went by the name of Chic, maybe because he had a pointy face and resembled a chicken. A blanket tip is the tip that had been negotiated in advance between the people who booked the convention and hotel management. I counted the money in the envelope I received when I returned to my sleeping quarters.

Two of my roommates, Joe and Ed, were lying on their bunks and talking. I sat on my cot, and as the conversation turned to the convention that had just finished, Ed asked me how the money was on the convention that I had worked. I said that my envelope contained $17 in tips. He asked me who had handed me the envelope. I said Chic and, without missing a beat, he said, "The scumbag robbed you." I wanted very much to deny that this had happened. After all, I was supposed to be a smart guy from Brooklyn.

Anyway, I took the advice of both Ed and Joe, who told me, when I got back to the dining room, wait until Chic was alone, approach him and just ask how much the tip was supposed to be for the busboy for each person served.

After telling Chic that I felt I had not received enough in

the envelope, his first question was, who had told me that I had not received enough. I knew enough not to mention names. With a very disgusted look on his face, Chic dug into his pocket and handed me a $20 bill. I later learned that Chic fit the description of a mountain rat and was an addicted gambler. Money didn't mean much to Chic; he only knew how to gamble and how to steal.

A few years after this incident, I met a guy who had worked with me at the Concord. He told me that Chic had become a "paperhanger" and had been convicted of writing several thousands of dollars in bad checks.

As time went on, I got bored with the repetition and monotony of dining room work. Maybe it showed. One evening after working dinner, Bobbie, the woman who had given me the ride when I first arrived in town and who I was friendly with, invited me to a card game in the room of one of the waiters. When I arrived, a poker game was in progress. I was asked if I wanted to join. I wasn't that good a poker player, but I did have a pretty good idea of the game. After about an hour and a half, I had lost all the money I had on me, about $90. It did seem a bit peculiar to me that I had received three or four excellent hands, like straights and full houses, and on each occasion was beaten out.

Even though I knew the odds were against that happening, I began to attend this game regularly, which was where most of my earnings went. The same people won all the time. Some of the older guys who had been around a little more than me were themselves getting suspicious of the game. I had a bad feeling about the situation in that room and eventually just stopped going.

I began going to another game regularly where blackjack was played. I won often enough to keep me interested. I liked getting the bank, the action was fast and a player could clean up if he got a run of luck, since the odds favored the bank. One morning after the breakfast break, a story made the rounds about a fight that had taken place the night before at the poker game I had been attending prior to my switch to the blackjack game. My friend Seymour said that a character named David, one of the guys who I remembered won most of the time, was caught putting a "cooler" into the game. I felt as if I should have known what a "cooler" was, but asked Seymour anyway. He explained that when it was the cheater's time to deal, the cheater shuffled the cards and placed the deck on the table. The player on his right would cut the cards. The dealer would then pick the deck up, pivoting his body to distract the other players in some way with his right hand, like checking the money in the pot. At the same time, he would move his left arm just below the edge of the table so he could make a quick slight-of-hand switch for the "cooler," a pre-set deck held by his partner, sitting on his left. Seymour mentioned that a fight broke out when the cheater was caught by one of the other players. I learned why I had lost so often and that crooked poker games were not uncommon.

I had been working at the hotel for about three months and was becoming good at what I was doing. It was June and the busy season was approaching. We were catering to near-capacity crowds when I was assigned to work with an additional waitress. I was now working six tables, which doubled my income and made me feel twice as tired at the end of the day.

One afternoon after lunch, a husky man wearing a suit and tie came over to my station and introduced himself as Arnie Fector. He was an organizer in the waiters union. He handed me his business card and said there would be a beer party in town on Friday night that I might find interesting. By Friday night, though, I had forgotten about the party. While I was cleaning up after supper and getting ready to leave the dining room, a guy who I had seen around and knew as John came up to me and asked if I was going to the beer party. John said it would be fun and urged me to go. He said we could grab a shower and meet in an hour and he would drive me to the party. I agreed.

The union hall was in a large loft on the third floor of a commercial building with stores occupying the street level. The setup reminded me of one of the furnished rooms that my father and I had occupied on Main Street in Asbury Park before I moved to Brooklyn. As I looked the place over, I noticed that most of the people present were workers from the hotel. Being younger than most everyone at the meeting made me feel shy, but John was proving to be a great host, grabbing the glass out of my hand and refilling it every time I half-emptied it.

As the night progressed, the place filled up and I began to loosen up. Walking around, I noticed some people playing cards in what looked like a sociable game; others were dancing. There were a group of guys talking in one spot. As I got closer, I noticed Seymour in the group. He greeted me and asked how I was making out. I joked about doing a lot better since I gave up the poker game.

One of the guys in the group asked what poker game I had been playing. When I mentioned some of the regulars at the game, he told me that he was in the game the night the cheaters were caught. He asked how I had first found out about the game. When I told him that my friend, Bobbie, had invited me, he just smiled. I found out later that Bobbie, who I was still friendly with, was suspected by more than a few to have been a "steerer" for the game. I didn't believe that she would have knowingly brought players to a crooked game. To have been taken in by the first woman I met at the hotel was too much for me to accept. I thought that even if she was a steerer, she may not have known that there were cheaters in the game. How could the person who had given me a ride to the hotel when I first arrived in Monticello have done this to me?

At about 9:00 p.m., people were asked to quiet down so that the speaker could be heard. The place was really packed. A tall, well-dressed guy moved toward a platform in the front of the hall. As things quieted down, a man I recognized as the one who had given me his card stepped to the microphone and introduced the tall man as Ed Shamansky, Director of Organizing. As he began speaking in a loud voice, the room became very quiet. He spoke about the lousy working conditions at the hotel, like workers having to work seven days a week, having to serve American plan, meaning 3 meals each day, which makes for a nine hour day, payroll cheating, the leftover food that we were given to eat, and the crowded sleeping quarters. He talked about the contract the union was trying to secure from management. He made it sound pretty good. Immediately after he finished speaking, cards were given to those who had not yet signed for the union. I was sold and signed, as did several others.

The next morning while working breakfast, some of the other workers congratulated me. I felt as if I had made some new friends. People I had not even known before began to greet me as we passed each other on our way to and from the kitchen. John, the guy who had driven me to the meeting, mentioned that I should talk it up for the union when I had a chance. Instead of being taken advantage of, as some people had said would happen to those who were in support of the union, I felt I was getting more respect. Scotty even told me that he was thinking of having me broken in as a waiter after the summer season when it slowed down.

I'd already saved up enough money and wanted to buy a car as soon as I learned to drive. I even had a few dates around that time and was losing some of my shyness. At times, I would get really gloomy, which was hard for me to understand. I discussed my feelings with Seymour, who I thought was a smart guy. He said he thought I was working hard and should probably take some time off after the union election, which was to take place in about a month. Actually, the election and the end of the summer season came at about the same time, around Labor Day. We won the election, which gave us the right to be union workers and to negotiate a decent contract. I was glad and liked my little union book. It really made me feel grown up. When I told Irving, the headwater, that I wanted some time off, he laughed and added his brand of wise guy humor. "What's the matter? The union wearing you out?" He asked how long I wanted off and I said I wasn't sure. We agreed that I would have a place if I wanted to return.

That Sunday after I collected my tips, I left quietly after saying goodbye to a few of my co-workers. I think I felt a little embarrassed at not having a good excuse for leaving, but I felt as if I had some unfinished business waiting for me back in New York. And in New Jersey, too. Perhaps it was the way my mother had died, or the way my father never explained to me what really happened. Or perhaps it was my old yearning for a real family. The friends I'd made at the hotel seemed to have revived that yearning, especially after I joined the union. I even thought of going back to high school, but I really didn't want to ask my father for support and didn't have much confidence in my academic potential. I knew I could have asked my brother Meyer, who was now working for Dumont Television Company as a highly respected electrical engineer, for help, and he probably would have given it to me, but I was ashamed to ask. I think my pride got in the way. Looking back, I think I made the right decision by not back-watering and accepting where I was at.

Real family. What was that like? What did it mean? Was it even possible for me to have that?

I left for New York unsure about everything and hopeful for something. I didn't know what.

Chapter 11: Knock Around Kid

The first thing I did when I got back to Brooklyn was to go to the room my father was living in and drop my bag off. While waiting for him to come home, I experienced a feeling that was new to me. Without having much to show for the five months that I had been working in hotels, I felt a sense of insecurity that was making me fearful. I felt as if I were a failure as a person. I knew that my brothers, whom I had not been in touch with since quitting high school, would certainly not be satisfied with me. I was also out of touch with my brother and sister on my mother's side and feeling like an outcast. I tried to tell myself that I didn't care about any of those people, including my father, but I did care and would have liked some kind of family warmth and approval.

At about 7 o'clock I went out for a sandwich. When I got back, my father was sitting in the room, waiting for me. He began asking me questions about why I hadn't kept in touch and what I had been doing. At first, I liked telling him about my experiences. But as he became critical of me I became defensive. We started to argue about my quitting the job at the Concord. Even though I thought he was right, I resented being told anything by him. I developed a feeling of deep hostility toward my father; a feeling I had never felt before toward anyone in my life. What had started out as my expectation of having a pleasant, man-to-man reunion with my father ended with me walking out of the room, trying to hide my tears as a failed man four months short of my 18th birthday.

As I walked down the steps and out to the street, the sweltering city heat seemed to place a timely emphasis on my new predicament. I had 65 bucks in my pocket and 110 bucks in a bank in Monticello, New York. There was no way I was going back to the furnished room I had been sharing with my father, except to get my few belongings. I was scared, but wouldn't admit it, not even to myself. I wasn't really thinking rationally, my anger was too intense and too diffuse. I was angry about everything and everyone around me.

I walked for a while without any real destination in mind. Eventually I saw some of the guys I knew from the neighborhood. They greeted me, asking how was I doing and where had I been? One joker gave the usual New York refrain, hollering, "What? You just get outta jail?" That got everyone laughing. Even I laughed and felt a bit cheered up. As I was caught up on neighborhood news, I learned that the poolroom that had been a hotspot for sports gambling was closed down because of a crackdown on illegal gambling that was sweeping New York.

I noticed that most of the regulars had stopped coming to the corner. I went into the cafeteria for coffee with the four or five still around. After catching up on their lives, I mentioned that I had had an argument with my father and needed a place to stay. A guy we called Bam told me that one of the roomers at his place had just been drafted into the army and the landlady had a "room to let" sign posted outside the house. I could probably have the room. I asked how much the rent was and he told me that he was paying $20 a month. Anyway, it was late and he said it would be all right for me to sleep in his room, I could talk with the landlady in the morning. I slept in his room that night, but didn't really like the place. In the morning, I thanked him and asked if I could show my appreciation by treating him to breakfast. At breakfast the first question I asked was where he learned to play three-cushion billiards so well. He had the reputation of being one of the best in the neighborhood. "Practice the right thing and not the wrong thing," he said. He added that this saying only worked for him in billiards. Bam was about 40 years old at the time. As our conversation went on I began to see there was a whole lot more to Bam's life than I had thought. Up until now I had only seen him around the poolroom and the corner. Though he was a small guy, people knew not to get on the wrong side of him. I later learned that he kept a German Luger side arm pistol that he had brought back from Germany after the war that he would use if he had to.

I was really surprised to hear about his experience in the European theatre during World War II. He married a French woman he met in Europe after the war. Each time I asked about some of the action he had been involved in, the conversation reverted back to Julie, his beautiful war bride, and their seven year old son whom he hadn't seen in a year. The child was living in Atlanta, Georgia, with his mother and her husband. At this point I followed the advice my father had given some years before and didn't ask any more questions. As time went on Bam and I became good friends. I learned that he had a disability pension from the Army, he was making ends meet by hustling a little pool and billiards, and he was a really great gin rummy player.

After breakfast we shook hands and he wished me luck. I walked around the neighborhood, looking at a few "room to let "signs posted in front windows of residential houses.

I felt shy about approaching any of the places, but finally got the nerve to ring a bell in one house that had a sign on the front door. A woman opened the door. When I told her I was interested in the room, she very graciously showed me two rooms which she had vacant, the smaller one for $18 dollars a month, the larger for $20. I asked for the small room. She explained that there were no kitchen privileges, but I could warm up some water for tea or coffee. Also, no guests allowed. She asked me some questions about myself. I told her that I had been working in a hotel. She cut me off with a big laugh and said, "Okay, as long as you work, it's good already." I gave her the $18 and she gave me a key. I left to get my belongings.

I got to my father's room, as I had planned, after my father left for work. His landlady was a nice woman who seemed interested in what was happening to me and surprised when I told her I had gotten a room on my own. She knew her son, Gordie, had helped me get the job at the Concord and asked how things had gone up there. Not wanting to get into much conversation, I just said things were good, but I wanted to take some time off and get back to the city. When she appeared to feel bad about me leaving her house, I explained that I was tired of being with my father and wanted to be on my own. She asked for my new address, which I gave to her. We spoke more than we ever had in the past, and on this occasion she said that she would like me to come back and visit her and Gordie.

I lugged my trunk (my original camp trunk from Camp Wel-Met) and a few other things on the first trip to my new room. On the second trip I took my travelling bag, a very sharp Army Air Corps zipper bag that my brother Hymie had given to me. I was proud when I carried it, which eased the chore.

When I got back to my newly rented room, the landlady was sitting in the kitchen drinking coffee. She watched me bring my things in and then asked me to sit down and have a cup of coffee with her. I was feeling the kind of shyness that made me disoriented, and said that I didn't want anything. Insisting that I sit down for a while, she talked about the butcher shop that her husband used to own and about her sons who lived in Detroit. Growing bored, I abruptly got up and left. At this point in my life, parting company abruptly was about the only thing that I was good at. It just came natural to me.

Since the poolroom on Livonia Avenue was closed, I went to another one nearby on Dumont Avenue, where I was surprised to see some of the habitués from the old place hanging out there. The name of the new spot was 'Marty,' the name of the owner. Marty was also a bookie who stopped his gambling operation when he was warned by the authorities from downtown, avoiding being closed down like many other poolrooms. His joint was just a little darker and seedier and had older pool tables with a lot of cigarette burns on the wood frames, like the same picture as the Livonia Avenue joint, but with a different frame.

I thought of playing, but wanted to conserve my money, since I only had about $45 in my pocket, had no job and was on my own. I sat down on a bench near one of the pool tables and just thought about my life. The feelings I was experiencing at the time were new and different. I felt as if I was in a trap. I felt alone and disconnected, but still desperate to prove that I was worth something. So far, at the ripe old age of 17, I knew I hadn't had much success. I had a vague idea at the time that I was fast becoming a bum. But I also think I was feeling excitement that maybe something would come out of my new life style.

In the days that followed, I would get up very late, hang out in the neighborhood for a while, then head uptown to Manhattan where I thought the real action was. There were a string of poolrooms along Broadway that were open all night, such as Aimes, Mcguires, 7-11 and, downtown on 14th Street, Julian's. These places were frequented for the most part by decent working people who were recreational players. The places had better tables and were kept cleaner by attendants than the Brooklyn poolrooms. Aimes and Mcguires even had rackers who racked the balls together after each game and were tipped by the players.

However, after midnight, when regular working guys left and the crowd thinned out, a group of hustlers and con men appeared who made side bets on the pool and 3-cushion billiard games. Some of these guys went by their real names, while others went by nicknames, like Barney the Horse, because he drove one of the recreational Hansom carriages around central park. Another guy was called The Lawyer because he gave advice to some of the petty swindlers who frequented the late night spots. They even started calling me The Kid, but I stayed away from these guys as Bam had cautioned me.

There were some excellent players who only got into a game when they gave up sufficient odds, spotting the opponent enough points to make the game seem enticing, but usually leaving enough of a margin for them to win. The advantage of playing or betting with these guys was that they always carried a sizable amount of money and had backers, so those who made smart bets could make a score. They were sometimes accused of "dumping," which meant throwing the game. It didn't take long to learn who the honest players were and who the cheats were, but, after my first week, I was broke. I told Bam, who I often hung out with, about my predicament. He said he thought that I could get the $100 that I had in the bank upstate by going to one of their local branches. I did and was able to withdraw my money after convincing a few of the bank officials that I was the right person.

With only 100 bucks in my kick, I knew I was going to have to begin earning some money. Bam said it might be a good idea if I got a job. I knew I could handle a resort waiter's job, but I was really turned off hotel work at the time. There were a lot of players in the neighborhood pool-room who played for money that I thought I could beat, so I tried my hand at hustling. On Friday night at about 6 p.m., a guy who I had seen around came in to Marty's poolroom. I had an idea that my game was a bit stronger than his, so I asked him to play. We started off by playing for small stakes, but as time passed and I began winning I asked for the stakes to be raised, which he agreed to. After about an hour I was ahead about $40 and he said that he was broke. I had won his whole week's salary, which didn't bother me at the time, but in looking back it was one of the worst things I have ever done, and I regret it to this day. I paid for the table time, washed my hands, and sat down on a bench.

I was in a place I really didn't want to be and wasn't going to get out of easily. I did whatever I had to do to exist. When I had money I spent it or gambled it, and when I was broke I borrowed bucks and deuces from the local guys, always giving them a time when I would repay the loan. I thought that telling them when I would repay the loan would make them feel more secure and more like-ly to spring. Anyway, it became hard for me to repay the loans and even harder to get them. I felt like I was in a hole trying hard to get out, but I kept slipping on the way up.

One night after the poolroom closed I went to Barry's Cafeteria, the local hangout on Saratoga and Livonia Avenues, and sat down with my friend Bam. Barry's was a well-lit place with the traditional long cafeteria counter where a few workers served food and punched a card, which the customers took when they entered the place and paid when they left. We usually got the food that had been laying around too long to have a really fresh taste, but it was okay.

As he learned more about my predicament, Bam again suggested that I get a job. When I told him I didn't want to do steady work, he told me about the agencies on Warren Street in Manhattan that had a lot of temporary jobs. I lost no time in going down to Warren Street the next morning.

After getting off the subway at Warren Street I walked up and down the street, not really knowing where I was. I eventually asked some person where the employment agencies were. He smiled as if to say, "Happy job hunting – you'll need it!" and pointed in the direction of several buildings across the street. I walked up to one of the buildings, looked inside and saw groups of men and women, dressed in work clothes, looking at the bulletin boards in front of the many employment agencies on the ground floor. The bulletin boards listed jobs being offered by the agencies. Some of the jobs listed didn't even exist, but were used to make the offices look like busy places. Once, I asked about a job that was listed and was told it had just been filled.

After checking out the ground floor, I went up to the first floor and learned that there were four floors of offices in this building and more of the same type of employment agencies in other buildings on the block. These agencies hired workers for various industries and specialized in low paying, mostly unskilled jobs, like waiter, day laborer, hod carrier, and temporary construction work. As time went on, I learned that these agencies had a reputation for being run by the sleaziest bunch of bloodsuckers one could encounter. Though these licensed thieves made poolroom hustlers look like choir boys, they were seldom reported to the authorities because many of the workers were recent arrivals who were unaware of their rights.

Once I saw a guy walk into an office and, without losing a beat, state, "If I don't get my $3 back, I'm going to turn every desk in this fuckin' office over." The agent gave the $3 up in a heartbeat. I don't know what had happened between the agent and the worker, but I do know these places often gave out phony jobs, hoping the ticket holder might not want to come back or might not have the train fare or maybe forgot where the place was located.

A small fee of $2 or $3 could secure a one-day job with the possibility of longer periods of work. Seeing a waiter job on one of the boards, I went into the office and asked one of the guys at a desk about the job. He explained that the job was lunch work in a club frequented by lawyers and judges and that the tips were pretty good. The lunch was between 11 am and 3pm, which allowed time for setting up and cleaning up. Although I had never worked in a club, I had been a busboy at the Concord hotel and had done work as a relief waiter a few times on other people's day off after the union was formed, so I had a little experience and thought it was worth a shot.

I took a chance and paid the $2 to the agent in exchange for what was called a work ticket. I liked the idea that I didn't have to live in the cellar of a hotel to wait on tables, as is often the case at resorts. The address of the place and the name of the captain to see when I got to the place were written on the ticket.

At the club I was so nervous, my knees were wobbling as I started work. I don't know how I remained standing. But once the action began I managed to get through the lunch without much trouble, although I am sure they knew that I hadn't had much experience. Eventually, I became pretty good at club work, which wasn't really difficult because there were only a few entrée choices, coffee and dessert. I continued to frequent these agencies, but only when I was broke and desperate and had gambled away my last dollar.

At one point I became tired of waiting tables and saw what looked real good to me under the construction listing: "Laborer 2 day's work –$3 an hour." This was good money. I went into the office and asked for the job. I learned that to get construction work, I had to see the foreman of the job, who was seated at one of the desks. I walked up to him and told him I wanted the job for two days. He asked whether I had ever carried hod before and whether I was strong and how old I was. I said I was strong and that I was 19 and had carried hod. I thought to myself, "What the hell kind of a job is this anyway?"

He said, "Okay, I'll try you." He told me to go sit down, that we would be leaving in a few minutes and he would take care of my ticket, which meant that he would pay the agent fee and take it out of my check. I found a newspaper on one of the chairs and read it until the foreman, who some of the guys knew as Dom, called us to leave with him. After about an hour, he had gathered nine guys.

When we all went downstairs Dom piled us into a large truck and we headed out. I couldn't see where we were going because it was an enclosed truck. I was a little apprehensive, but figured we were headed in the right direction.

About thirty minutes later we arrived somewhere out in one of the boroughs at a big broken down building that Dom called "the location". I was trying to see what they were doing with the bricks when Dom shouted, "Now listen up! Youse guys will be loading bricks in bags from the inside of the site and bringing them to the table to be cleaned. It's really easy and you'll be shown how to do it.

After the bricks are cleaned, the carriers will bring them in big bags to the truck and load them on."

He then asked which of the guys had ever done cleaning before. I think about five said they had and he told them to work the table. He then brought the other four of us inside the building, which was broken down, had a smell of wet junk and was very dilapidated. He showed us which bricks were good enough to be loaded in our bags and which ones were too broken up to be salvaged.

So there I was for the day, loading hundred-pound bags from inside the building and bringing them to the table, and carrying hundred-pound bags from the table and loading them on the truck. One of the guys asked me if I had ever carried hod before. I said yes. Not much more conversation took place for the rest of the day on my end, but I learned that what I was doing was called "hod lugging" and made a mental note to ask in a clearer way what I would be doing next time I went out on a job. Actually the job wouldn't have been bad if there hadn't been one guy at the building hollering, "Let's go! Let's go!" all day and another guy at the table hollering, "Move it!" I couldn't resist asking at one point, "Let's go where?" That got a smile from the foreman who answered, "Wise guy!"

It was hard to screw off, but I did sometimes examine the bricks for a few long moments just to get my wind. I was exhausted and fell asleep for most of the long subway ride back to Brooklyn. Even though the work was hard, I was glad to go back again to make another day's pay. At 2 p.m. the next day we were told the job was over, but if we stayed in touch with the agency, there would be more work down the line. We were paid for 15 hours, which gave me a grand total of $45.

As I walked to the subway in the Bronx, my back was caving in, my legs buckling under, and my feet aching, but my spirits were good and 45 bucks in my pocket could buy me a lot of action, win or lose.

Whenever I ran out of money, I would go back to the agencies and check out what work was available at the time. Some of these jobs provided a way to pick up the basics of a trade. I liked painting, but never got into much more than rough work using the big roller. Window frames and molding was done by the regulars, not the agency extras.

Sometimes I would make the Washington Markets shape up, which was a little bit of a spin on the system. You would go down to the Washington Markets, which were wholesale outlets located on West Street in downtown Manhattan. Usually about fifty to one hundred men stood in a large open space by the market where the trucks bringing produce from all over the country had to be unloaded. The boss stood on a platform and picked men from out of the group, usually the guys he knew would kick back 5 dollars for a night's work. Before being assigned to unloading you had to say "who you were with," which told him who he had to split the kickback with for sending you to the shape up.

I never knew who all the sources were, but I did know that some of the guys came from wise guy social clubs around the city. In my case, the kickback went to one of the agencies that I knew enough to mention.

The night's work consisted of walking in a line with a leader who set the pace in a gang of six or seven guys. When each guy reached the front of the line, he picked up a box, which wasn't light, and walked seven or eight feet to place the box on a skid.

Porters would then come from the markets during or after the bidding to load hand trucks or small carts with the boxes of produce which had been purchased by retail market proprietors. The porter's job was better because it was steady, they made good tips and they were members of the stevedore's union.

I had mixed feelings about the shapeup, mainly because I didn't like the hours. It was a good workout once you got used it and the money wasn't bad, fifteen dollars after the kickback for seven hours of work with one thirty minute break.

I liked going to breakfast at a waterfront diner after work and listening to the guys talk about all the usual things that marginal working class guys are concerned about. It was a lot like street stream of consciousness, or maybe should be called street of consciousness real life stories. I had a lot of respect for these guys because of the mixture of stubbornness and strength that guided their lives like a reed that would bend but not break.

Making money, whether by gambling or working, gave me a lift, but things never seemed to improve much. Most of the time, I was depressed. As my disposition became more nasty and abrasive, I had fewer and fewer friends. I got into altercations and was becoming antisocial. Those who I considered my friends were drug addicts and people who had done time in prison. I smoked marijuana and tried small shots of heroin by injection a couple of times. My father tried to contact me on a couple of occasions, but I stayed out of touch with him, as well as with my brothers Hymie and Meyer. I had no contact with my other brother Julius or my sister, Eleanor.

Marty, the owner of the poolroom, told me more than once that the Army would be a good place for me, since the Korean War was now over. I thought about this a lot and finally decided to volunteer for induction after I turned 19. I went to the draft board and asked to be moved up on the list. After the physical examination, I was classified 1A. A few months later I received my greetings for induction. I said good-bye to the few whom I considered my friends and took the subway to Whitehall Street in downtown Manhattan, the site of the induction center and the departure point to Fort Dix where I would receive my basic training.

Chapter 12: You're In The Army Now

The day was March 22, 1954. I arrived at the induction center in time to get on the bus at 9 a.m., headed for Fort Dix, New Jersey. The New Jersey Turnpike hadn't yet been built. I remember seeing highway signs pointing to familiar places, like Asbury Park, which made me feel a little nostalgic and excited about the things to come. I think what I was experiencing on this morning was confidence that I was now making a new and better turning point. For the past ten years, ever since coming to foster care in Brooklyn, I had not been happy. On the bus ride, I found myself identifying with my brother, Hymie. My memories of when Hymie left our home to go to the Army Air Corps were strong. Still, there was one big difference. He was going to serve as World War II was beginning and I was going just a few months after the Korean War had ended.

When the bus arrived at Fort Dix we were taken to our assigned barracks and told what mess hall to eat at. By the time I found the mess hall I was really hungry and asked whether I could have seconds. The guy in the white cook's outfit looked at me in a strange way and said yes, but added that this was the mess hall that fed new inductees - not many guys ever asked for seconds. The greasy pork chops, lumpy mashed potatoes and soggy string beans tasted pretty good.

The next day we were issued a full set of GI clothes and went to the medical team for our shots. Eight medics with long needles gave us our injections to a form of cadence designed to keep the line moving at a brisk speed.

In true 1950's Army tradition, these guys endured the injections with a Roman stoicism. I figured they must have been truck drivers or ranch hands in civilian life, they never even winced at the needle.

Next began two months of basic training. I got into real good shape and probably would have liked it if it weren't for the harassment I was subjected to. I soon learned harassment was a part of Army life for new inductees, but I was never quite sure if I wasn't getting a little more than average because of my abrasive personality. On the second day, while standing at attention in our newly issued fatigues and in full company formation, our platoon was answering the roll call when my name was called. Well, I had always liked my name, Maron, to be pronounced correctly. On this morning our field first sergeant, Sgt. Prince, who hailed from Tennessee and was in charge of all training, pronounced my name "May-ron." I immediately shouted the correct way of saying my name. I guess I was getting a little cocky at this point, after all the good chow, nice clothes with shiny brass buttons, good leather high boots, a clean place to sleep with plenty of guys to talk to, even a few Brownsville guys. I felt I had found a home, until my fatal flaw of correcting Sgt. Prince's pronunciation of my name. The next thing I heard was a loud and clear blast of a voice with a southern twang shout out: "The only voice I want to hear in this formation is my own! Drop down and give me 25 pushups, May-ron!" I did the pushups without much trouble, which I think surprised Sgt. Prince. Next time I screwed up, he ordered thirty-five.

Basic training was tough for everyone, especially for me. My problem with accepting authority just wouldn't go away. I made up my mind to try a little harder, because I wanted to stay in the military. Our cadre of trainers had all served in Korea only a short time before and I suspect some were afflicted with Post Traumatic Stress Disorder, but this diagnosis was not yet in effect in1954. It was called "battle fatigue." Soldiers returning from combat were told that it would go away in a short time.

Basic training was taken very seriously, with only a little ongoing comic relief, which took the form of a competitive battle between Sgt. Prince and my platoon leader, Sgt. Booth. Prince gave the impression of being a jovial redneck type of guy, good natured most of the time. Sgt. Booth was a dignified black man who hailed from New York. There was always some form of bickering between these two men, even on the field and sometimes in front of our entire company in training. During a double time order as the whole platoon jogged in cadence, Sgt. Prince started picking on Sgt. Booth, telling him to "move his lard ass." Sgt. Booth told Prince he could kiss his "lard ass" as we all laughed, which got Prince pissed. He threatened to kick Booth's ass. Booth then told him it wouldn't be a good idea because then he wouldn't be healthy enough to even kiss his ass.

Sometimes these guys reminded me of my junior high school teachers. I think they really liked each other and were having fun and this was just their way of fighting boredom. I did have an attitude problem and spoke back to superiors a little too often, but I survived the drills. I never did so many punishing pushups for being what is commonly referred to in military language as a "fuckup," but they put me in shape. Taking all the shit was something I needed to learn and probably gave me an edge on character building.

After infantry basic training, I was sent to cook and baker school at Fort Dix for my second eight-week cycle, where I learned to follow army recipes and became one of the fastest fried egg and pancake makers in the class, which landed me an assignment in an artillery outfit somewhere near downtown Philadelphia in the Cobbs Creek section, adjacent to a golf course. I guess we were supposed to be protecting the golfers. I never found out much about 90 millimeter cannons, since I was assigned to work in the mess hall. After being introduced to the mess sergeant, everything was fine for about the first 15 minutes of our working relationship. He liked to talk about his German wife. I found this part interesting, until he started telling me how he thought that Hitler was misunderstood by Americans and that he had really done a lot for the German people. He liked to criticize different ethnic styles of seasoning food. He always told one of our kitchen staff , a corporal from Yauco, Puerto Rico, that Spaniards "like you" like to put too much hot sauce on everything. He would tell another cook named Sereno that Italians used too much tomato sauce. And me he told Jews overload everything with vinegar and love pickled foods.

I found his highly opinionated and bigoted outlook obnoxious. After about two months, when it became obvious to people around us that we were on the verge of coming to blows, I was called into the first sergeant's orderly room. His first question was why I didn't like the mess sergeant and what the problem was between us. I told him Sgt. Freed was a prick. I really thought he would want more of an explanation or maybe get mad, but he just broke out in laughter as he opened the bottom draw of his desk and pulled out some papers. As he grabbed for his phone, I wasn't sure what was coming off, but when I heard him ask for some captain in the food unit, I had an idea. When the captain got on the phone he explained that he had a good man for his unit and said I would fit in. After a little more small talk, he said he would send me the next morning. I liked the exchange, especially when the first sergeant answered a question by saying, "Yes, he's a hard worker."

As soon as he got off the phone, he told me that he was sending me for temporary duty to the food distribution center at Valley Forge Army Hospital. He said it would be like a regular job. I wondered why he didn't ask if it was alright with me when I remembered that I was now in the Army and not in some employment agency where you negotiate for a job. I even felt as if I had just quit my job and had been given another one more to my liking. He told me not to mention where I was going and to take a pass and go to town and be ready to be picked up at 8 am the following morning. I didn't know if I should salute on my way out, so I did, and as he dropped his arm I can still hear his last words to me. "Stay out of trouble and do your best."

The next morning the driver came on time and the ride was pleasant. The driver told me where Valley Forge Army Hospital was, when it was built and a few other short details. He said it was a good duty. After arriving at the hospital I was assigned to a dormitory with other men who were all non-commissioned officers and worked on all kinds of jobs, from occupational therapists to military police. There were also some other food workers. The hospital was big and gave me the impression of a place where people's lives had been put back together. I saw people moving in all directions dressed as patients or medical workers and smelled the typical hospital medicinal smells mixed with the scent of cafeteria, delights the likes of which I hadn't yet seen in military life. I felt I was doing something important.

After getting set up with a bunk and a metal closet in a dormitory loft with about twenty other men, I went to the food warehouse I had been assigned to. A corporal sitting at a desk in the main office asked for my assignment papers. He told me to take a seat outside and said he would be right with me. After a few minutes he came out and said we'd go for a walk around the place and then he would introduce me to the man I'd be working for. As we walked, he showed me where the trucks were unloaded and where the food was stored until it was picked up by distribution trucks that came from different outfits in the area. He pointed to the skids where the food was placed for distribution.

When we got to the back of the warehouse, I saw a guy with three stripes on his arm and a slight beard, which I thought was considered out of uniform and not permitted. There were a bunch of papers in his hand and a higher bunch of papers on a desk in front of where he was standing. The guy showing me around said this sergeant was in charge and was a pretty good guy. We spoke for a few minutes as he explained that a lot of trucks were making drop offs today. I was assigned to unload the truck as the boxes came off a long runner.

I got a pretty good workout that first day. Since I had arrived late, I only worked about two hours in the morning and then went to lunch, where a really great chow was served. There was a much better grade of food than we had at the artillery base. The cafeteria was situated inside the main building of the hospital with actual choices of main dishes, soups, and tasty desserts, all in a co-ed, friendly environment. If patients were well enough to eat outside their rooms, they were served the same food and were given help when needed. After lunch I usually worked about 4 or 5 hours, depending on where I was needed. Most of the details were pretty simple and repetitious, except for filling orders, which took some judgment. Each of about thirty artillery outfits in the area submitted requests for what they needed until the next distributions, usually three or four days apart. If a specific item was ordered, it might not be available at the time and a substitution had to be made. Substitutions were often made into jokes, like, "Can I substitute cranberry sauce for turkey or bacon for eggs?" We did a lot of good work at the warehouse and had some fun, but most of the guys were draftees like me and looked forward to getting out. When one became what was called a short-timer, they always started counting the days and the hours and became happy.

After chow was finished at night I would often hang out in the recreation room and play chess and sociable games of pool with patients or staff. Somehow I acquired the nickname "Brooklyn" and was sometimes asked to settle differences that occurred in pool games, especially in eight ball, which was the most popular pool game, with somewhat confusing rules. I knew that house rules changed from venue to venue. I never found out what rules were used at the hospital, so I developed a set of rules, wrote them out and posted them on the wall. One of the most confusing of these rules was what is done if one makes all the striped or solid color balls but is blocked by another ball which is in front of the eight ball. I still don't know exactly, but I established the shooter does not lose and gets another opportunity to shoot at the eight ball. A lot of the guys were amazed at how strong my pool game was. I never told them about the fact that I practically lived in a poolroom before the Army.

After a couple of months I enrolled for driving lessons. I wanted more of a social life than I was having and thought of buying a car. I got my license and bought an old Dodge for $250. I used it until it died a week before my discharge. I always liked driving into Philadelphia because there were many great jazz clubs, several with top line performers. You could see Billy Holliday or Sarah Vaughn at the Showboat or Blue Note and you didn't have to spend much more than the price of a drink at the bar. That was old Philly!

One morning I met a nice nurse named Mary. My friend Jack Connor and I were talking about the show we had seen the night before at one of the clubs. Jack was a guy who lived in Germantown, a suburb near Philly, and he really knew the town. Sometimes when we went in together, we would go to after-hours clubs. These clubs had everything, from poetry to gambling and dancing with no holds barred. After we chatted a bit more Jack excused himself and left. As I was finishing my coffee, Mary, who was sitting across from us, explained that she wanted to know about the music scene in Philly. I told her as much as I knew, which, was mostly the jazz places. She told me she would love to go to a jazz club, but always had too many drinks when she went out. I volunteered immediately to accompany her, which was the only thing I ever volunteered for during my two-year stint in the military. We made an appointment to meet at chow the next evening, dressed in our civvies, and go out straight from there.

After chow we walked toward the parking lot, where I offered to take my car, but she said she would like to drive to get used to the directions. As we walked toward her car I was kind of glad that I didn't have to take my junk heap and wondered what she was driving. I was very surprised as we approached her 1954 Thunderbird. Mary loved her car. The first thing she told me was that she had always wanted a Thunderbird, but couldn't afford it until recently.

She said she hadn't been home to Atlanta with her new car, but her parents were sure to be impressed because she said her dad loved cars. We made good time and parked downtown, where we checked out a few of the clubs and decided on a later show at The Blue Note starring Ella Fitzgerald and a good back-up group. The club had a nice mahogany bar, soft lights and a slightly raised stage. We weren't too hungry, so we shared a sandwich and ordered drinks. Mary was right, she was a little looped after only two drinks, so I drove back. I tried to be cool, as if I drove Thunderbirds every day, but I don't think I could hide how happy I was to be part of what I considered a really hip scene. When we got back to the hospital I walked her to the cutoff point of the women's quarters, where we hugged and said we would go out again.

A few weeks later Mary wanted to visit Brooklyn, my home town. I tried to explain that I really didn't have a family to visit. She wanted to visit the borough anyway, so we drove to Coney Island and had a fun weekend in New York. After we had a few drinks and hot dogs at the famous Nathan's in Coney Island I got a tattoo at her suggestion.

A few weeks later Mary was transferred to Walter Reade in Washington, DC. Two months later she wrote and told me she had met the most wonderful MD and that she was sending me an invitation to the wedding. No thanks.

Although I had overcome a good part of my shyness and anger, I still often felt depressed and lonely. But the people I was around were good for me. I had a few friends during my 14 months of duty at the hospital. I did notice some people who had developed close relationships while serving at the hospital and was glad for them, but I don't think I was ready for anything more than casual fun – it was all I could handle.

Working at the hospital was good duty. The food was good, the people were nice, and it was like a regular job with weekends off. I met Eddie Brione in the rec room playing pool and we soon became friends. I found out that Eddie's main interest in life was horse racing. He was a good-looking, wiry, guy from Lexington , Kentucky who knew a lot about horses. Eddie knew about breeding, training, blood lines and a lot more, but his main interest was the business of horse racing. Studying the horse racing results in the newspaper, he said had a system he could use to beat the odds and bragged about how much he would have won if he had been at the race track.

I kept telling Eddie that it was impossible to always win, since the odds were against the bettor from the start. I said that yes, a bettor could have a good day at the track, but, over time the bettor would wind up with a bunch of losing tickets while the track wound up with all the money. We both agreed that if we knew of any fixed races or any doped horses, we could be big winners, but that wouldn't happen, the larceny going on was only known to the inside crowd: the jockeys, owners, and trainers, but not the average suckers.

One day, we made a deal. I said I would book his bets for a week. We made a $20 bet on who would come out ahead at the end of the week. Eddie wanted to pick his choices from any track listed in the Morning Telegraph, the official racing journal. I wanted the choices limited to fewer tracks. We finally agreed that he would have a choice of three tracks on any of the six days during our bet. At the end of the week, Eddie had lost about $200 on paper making me the winner of our $20 bet.

That was just the beginning for me. I began looking in Eddie's racing journals and making what was referred to in the Brooklyn poolroom as "mind bets." In other words, make-believe bets where no money was wagered and none changed hands. These mind bets turned to "if bets" which were, "if I were at the track I would bet on" this horse or that horse. This was the beginning of my horse betting interest that, fortunately, never turned to a serious addiction, although I did lose money.

When we had weekend passes, Eddie and I frequently spent our time at New Jersey and Pennsylvania race tracks. Thanks to our friendship, I spent the last year of my tour of duty broke most of the time. But Eddie was a lively guy with a big Southern accent to match my Brooklyn accent. When we did win, we went to Philly and had a good time.

Once we stopped in at the Betty Mills Exotic Bar, a topless club in Philly. After a few shots of my favorite drink, Seagram's 7 and soda, I got into a conversation with one of the dancers just as the club was closing. Somehow, I woke up the next morning in bed with two women, one of whom was bouncing very high up and down on the bed mattress. She was a very small person, the size of a doll, with a pretty face. The other woman in the bed had the strong build of a farm girl, but very curvy and feminine. When the strong woman asked the tiny woman to stop jumping, they started arguing, the strong woman calling the tiny woman "a midget." After a few minutes things quieted down and took a totally different course, which felt much better than the bouncing.

I remembered that the night before I had seen the picture of a woman dancer in the topless bar, Mable the Marvelous Midget. Gradually, the night before came back to me and I realized I was in bed with two of the dancers from the show at the Betty Mills Exotic Bar.

After a shower and a cup of coffee, I discovered that my pass was overdue. Knowing I was AWOL, I said I had to leave. They both protested, saying the "little pimp" was coming to take their money and wanted me to keep that from happening. Even though I was now AWOL, I decided to stay a little longer and see what would happen with the pimp. I took a look in my wallet and noticed that I had about $50 less than I should have had, even with what I had spent in the bar the night before. At least, Mabel and her friend had left me some money. I didn't make an issue of it, since I had had a good time.

At around 4:00 in the afternoon, I realized that I was now probably in serious AWOL trouble and said I had to go. Mabel the Marvelous Midget started to cry. She said the pimp was going to get there soon and take their money for sure, so I stayed another hour. I asked strong woman if they had a baseball bat in the house. She came back with a four foot pipe. I asked her if she could swing it. She demonstrated a swing that could have put a dent in a concrete wall. At that point, I kissed them both and while running down the steps to catch the bus back to the base as soon as I could hollered, "I feel sorry for the little pimp!"

The next morning I went to my shift at the hospital warehouse. I had missed an afternoon of work. After telling the sergeant the truth about what had happened, he just laughed and I never heard any more about it. That night at the rec room while shooting pool I saw Eddie. He asked me where I had disappeared to when Betty Mills closed. He laughed so hard at the story he couldn't finish the game, and we remained friends until my day of discharge.

One afternoon as I was returning from lunch, my sergeant called me into his office and said he had an envelope for me. I couldn't imagine what it was or who had sent it. I opened it and saw a letter which congratulated me on my promotion to Private First Class. I was kind of happy because at least having one stripe was proof that

I had been around for a while and wasn't a fresh recruit. The sergeant told me the promotion came through from my former artillery outfit. I called Sgt. Kelly and thanked him for putting me in for promotion. He said he heard I was doing okay and had the time in for promotion, so he did what was right. He then asked how much time I had left in my hitch. When I told him about eight months, he asked if I was going to stay in the Army. Before I could say a word he told me about how he could hook me up with a Warrant Officer commission and all the benefits of the job. At the time I didn't know what a Warrant Officer did and still don't, but I didn't think it was a job I wanted. We both just laughed and wished each other luck and said good-bye. I never found out if he was joking about my future in the army.

Nobody in the warehouse noticed my new stripe. That evening at dinner I told my friend Tex about it. Tex, who was from Dallas and worked as an occupational thera-pist, made me feel as if the most wonderful thing in the world had happened to me. He hugged me and said that we had to celebrate my promotion, what was I doing with my weekend pass? When I told him I would be around, he said we should celebrate by going to the VFW in town and get plastered. I appreciated his sentiments, though I knew almost anything would provide a reason for Tex to get plastered.

It turned out things didn't really work out the way we thought they would. When we arrived at the VFW on Saturday afternoon, there was a bunch of guys and girls sitting around drinking beer. Tex didn't lose any time in telling everyone about our celebration. After another beer or two we decided that we'd buy a keg of VFW beer and go to a farmhouse to celebrate and play a game of softball.

When we started the game, I noticed that there were

always players missing from the infield and many switches were taking place as the innings went on. I think it was somewhere in the middle of the game, maybe the 4th or 5th inning, when a short, very round and pretty young woman asked me if I wanted to see a nice colt.

When I asked where the colt was, she pointed toward what looked like a barn way out on the grounds. As we walked to the barn, we made some small talk, and when we got to the barn I asked one of the dumbest questions I have ever asked. "Where's the colt?" After a few more minutes we were getting it on, not missing the colt at all. We stayed good friends and continued to see each other until my discharge. I even visited her a few times after my discharge, but, eventually we lost contact. I'm sure she's a beautiful grandmother now.

That's about it for Army life.

Chapter 13: A Stab At The Needle Trades

After receiving my separation papers and being honorably discharged from the army, I stayed with my father until I found my own place, which was a basement apartment in a nice house in the East Flatbush section of Brooklyn. The landlord didn't ask any questions and I didn't offer anything about myself except that I was recently discharged from the Army. I did see an elderly woman who I guess was his wife open a door one flight from where we were talking and take a quick look and nod, which must have been her approval. The rent was 30 dollars a month. I even had a phone installed, which was the first phone I ever had in my own apartment. I sure felt important.

I didn't want to start hanging out with the guys in the old neighborhood, but I did go to Marty's poolroom to hear some gossip and shoot a sociable game of pool. Having some money in my pocket, I did not even think of gambling. Thinking of buying a car, I looked in the used car section of the local paper, where I focused on a '53 Ford listed for 450 dollars. I called the owner, who drove the car to my house. When he arrived I was on the porch and went down to meet him. I didn't know much about cars, but did know that it would be a good idea to have a mechanic look the engine over. I asked if I could test drive the car, and he said I could. I told him that I knew a guy who was a mechanic and asked if we could go see the guy. When he didn't object I drove to the station and showed it to Mel, who I knew from JHS and who had gone to Brooklyn Automotive High School. We hadn't seen each other for a few years, so we talked a bit as he checked the car. When he finished he called me aside and asked how much the guy was asking for the car. I told him 450 and he said it was worth it, but that there were some marks on the body and it needed some paint touch up.

After offering the man 400 dollars I became the proud owner of a 1950 Ford. I could now travel in style. I realized that I needed to get a job. I was eligible for unemployment insurance as a newly discharged member of the military, but I knew if I got into that I would be where I was before going into the Army. This was not an appealing thought.

That night I went for supper to Pop's Inn, an old hangout on Saratoga Avenue near the Ambassador Movie Theatre. Pop's was still a good place for an inexpensive meal. It had the usual luncheonette format, with pictures of champion boxers and racehorses on the walls and a table where the local bookie always sat.

Not much had changed in the two years since I'd left, except that a few of the young ladies had filled out nicely. Maybe I just hadn't looked before. The food was good and the portions were filling.

Seeing a couple of guys I knew having supper at a table near the door, I asked if I could join them. As we talked I mentioned that I had been looking for a job, which was probably obvious since I was wearing a suit. A suit meant you were looking for a job, employed as a salesman, or going to a wedding. Arthur, who drove a truck, said that an embroidery place where he picked up goods had just let a salesman go and was probably looking to hire someone new. I took the name of the company from him and got their number from the telephone book. Though I was still shy, I was making an effort to overcome this problem. The fact that I had ambition helped.

I called the company, Holbrook Mills, about the possible job opening in sales. The person I spoke with asked some questions and said I could come by for an interview for the opening anytime between the hours of 9 and 5 o'clock on any workday.

When I got to the place the next day, I was expecting a big mill with many machines and a lot of noise, like the factories I had seen in the past. As it turned out, Holbrook Mills was a small two-room office in a rundown building on 33rd Street in the heart of the lingerie district. As I approached the office, I told a young woman sitting at a desk behind an open window that I had called and was told to come by for a job interview. She invited me in, said one of the bosses would be back soon and I could wait for him in the office. I sat down. She introduced herself as Rhoda. We chatted for a while about what kind of a company Holbrook was, but I really wasn't able to make much of a judgment since I had no understanding of the embroidery business. What I did get out of the talk was that it was a very small company recently started by two guys who had quit their jobs as salesmen to start their own company.

After about an hour the boss, Mr. Martin, arrived. Rhoda told him a little bit about me. He said he would be right with me. After about 15 minutes he invited me to sit down at his desk so that we could talk about what he called "the position." He introduced himself as Bob and said that he and his partner, Jerry, had started the company two years before. They had both been salesmen at the same embroidery company before starting their own operation. He said that I would be trained and taught about the product while working in the office, and that my duties would be to drive the truck and make deliveries, which he said was part of the learning process. He also made some promises about me being rewarded for my hard work and dedication to the growth of the organization. He said that as a trainee the pay was not much, but I was lucky to be entering at a wonderful time. He went on and on about the fabulous growth potential of the company. As we sat and talked, the other partner, Jerry, dropped in and said that he thought this was a great opportunity for someone who had just gotten out of the service. I felt motivated and took the job at a salary of $35 a week, wanting to believe everything Bob said. I was told to come in at nine the following morning.

When I arrived the next morning, neither of the two bosses were there, but Rhoda had just gotten in. She showed me some of the many embroidered fabrics that were used as trimmings on the ladies undergarments marketed by the lingerie trade. She explained how the raw cotton material, called "gray goods," came from the weaving mill in an off white color and had to be dyed white before it could be embroidered with their designs. The designs were not original, but were copied and changed by a designer to get around the copyright laws. The designs were simply stitched patterns, sometimes flowers or other ornamentations, embroidered on the garments to give them style. The company supplied primarily the foundations industry. Foundations was a fancy word for ladies brassieres and corsets, which supported tits and ass.

As the day progressed I was asked to make several deliveries and pickups around the city and began to wonder what my job really was. About three o'clock, when Jerry asked me to make another delivery he said that when I go to factories and outlets that we service I should introduce myself to the people there and make friends. He also instructed me not to get parking tickets on the truck because he said that they were expensive.

Jerry told me to make a delivery of flat goods to Maiden Form Brassieres, a factory in Long Island City. At the factory I brought in three boxes of the flat embroidered goods and introduced myself to several people who were present.

When I got downstairs I noticed a parking ticket on the truck. I looked at the ticket and noticed that it was issued for parking in a restricted area. When I left I drove around the block to see where I should have parked and noticed that all of the parking in the area was restricted until 6 p.m.

The next day when I saw Jerry he asked me what had happened and I told him about the ticket, which I had given to Rhoda. He said that I should have known better than to park in a restricted area, and that I had taken too long to make the delivery. He raised his voice and appeared upset.

This gave me a new problem to deal with for future reference. I had to learn to deal with my shyness while meeting new people and exchanging information about who was making what type of garment, all this while making fast deliveries. The people in the industry often wanted to know what their competitors were working on for the coming season. This was very important information appreciated by the manufacturers, but I didn't really dig being a corset/brassiere spy.

I was not good at what is now referred to as networking, but, as time went by I could not help meeting salespeople, designers, and people in the production end of the business. Through the natural course of events and basic social situations, I began to learn about the industry and that Jerry had a bad temper.

A factory in West New York, New Jersey, stitched the embroidery designs on the plain, flat cotton goods. Sometimes I would pick up the embroidered goods from the factory, which was the industrial center for the embroidery trade in the metropolitan New York area. This factory had several of the big Shifley machines. The machines were about 40 feet long with long metal spiral type bars. The machines operated on the same principal as the player piano, with a mechanical card feeder that would control the stitching process of these very noisy machines. This is all done by computer now and, for sure, no longer in this country. I usually arrived early with the truck and would hang around until the job was boxed and ready to go.

One day when I was there during the lunch hour a guy named Tony asked if I would like to go to lunch with him. We went to a restaurant bar on the corner by the mill. Our talk was really interesting. Tony was a Korean War veteran who had seen a lot of action and loved talking about his experiences, especially of his R&R in Japan.

He filled me in on the industry and its history, and told me things that I had not heard in the one month that I had been at Holbrook Mills, like my bosses were both assholes. I smiled and nodded in agreement.

When we finished our sandwich and beer I bought a round for us. At this point, things kind of loosened up a bit. He talked about how his boss sometimes sends him directly to the manufacturers to get business if his shop is in need of work. This was a way of cutting out the middle suppliers like us. Although he seemed good natured and jovial, he was a bitter guy.

When I told him that I was hoping to start selling soon and that I hoped to make some money, he laughed. When I asked why he laughed he said he wished me luck, but this was a competitive business based on friendship or favoritism. Most salesmen were pushing the same products that the buyers could buy from anybody. Once a determination was made on who to deal with, only the price had to be settled. He said at this point often the salesman was cut out of the deal by assholes like the guys I was working for.

As we were walking back from lunch he jokingly said that I would do well in the industry if I was ready to go to bed with fashion designers like my bosses were doing. I saw a lot of anger and some jealousy behind Tony's jokes, but I liked him. We went for a drink together when we had time. I found out that the anger Tony had toward my bosses was because the salesman I replaced was his friend. One of my bosses had made deals with accounts his friend had brought into the company behind his friend's back. This was flat out stealing the salesman's commission. I thanked him for sharing the information.

After about 3 months of delivery and truck driving I decided to approach the bosses about allowing me to start calling as a salesman. I had been given one $5 a week raise, but was having a problem making ends meet on just $40 a week. I had a car and was going to dances on Saturday nights and occasionally went on a date. Women were not sharing expenses at that time and I needed more money. When I explained this to Jerry and Bob, they both told me that I was not ready because I did not know enough yet. I argued that if I could make the proper contacts they could help me close the deals. I said that I had enough of an understanding of the industry to present myself intelligently and that the rest would come with practice. The discussion ended with me giving them one more month to let me start as a salesman.

When my day came to go out to the field, I donned my best and only suit and was given a book of samples, mostly old samples that we had used in the past. I was satisfied that the book was a good frame of reference for what we could produce, which I already knew was the same as everyone else in the trade was doing. I was given a typed list of about fifteen accounts that I should not go near under any circumstances, and was told that I could call on any other user or potential user. Both bosses wished me well, as did Rhoda.

Though a little self-conscious, over the next few months I began calling on buyers of all of the big companies. Sometimes they took my samples and asked a price. I always told them that I would work with them on the price. When I got back to the office each day, either Jerry or Bob always asked how I was doing and who I had called on. It wasn't long before I found that Bob was attempting to make contact with some of the accounts that I had tried to bring in and considered mine. When I told Bob that I heard from one of the production managers that he was trying to work out a deal with one of the companies I had given samples to, Bob explained that he had met this person by chance and began talking business with him. He said that if a deal was made, I would get all of the commission. I took his explanation in good spirit, but suspected it was bullshit.

Some afternoons around 4 o'clock, groups of salesmen would gather around, talk business, and gossip. I would sometimes hang out for a while, but was not really interested, except the time I heard a story making the rounds at the Sniffin Court Café on Madison and 36th about my boss, Bob.

Bob had met a dress model from Baltimore in one of the local watering holes and dated her a few times before setting her up in a Midtown Manhattan apartment. After having a falling out with her, he tried to stick her with the eight months that was left on the lease. When she protested, he told her she was a signatory to the lease and would have to pay. At that point she told Bob that her father wanted him to come down to Baltimore and discuss a real estate deal where a lot of money could be made. Bob took the bait. When he got to the Baltimore meeting place, he was greeted by the girl's father and a few of his friends. Her father told him if he didn't pay off the lease, he would have a very hard time walking in the near future.

In the end, Bob made good on the lease.

As time went on, I made a few sales, but, unable to get follow-up business or build up accounts, I soon became discouraged with the whole industry. I began to feel that I did not have the type of personality that lent itself to small talk and schmoozing, and that I wasn't really interested very much in who sold embroidery or coverings for tits and ass.

I began hanging out with some of my old friends. Most of those guys couldn't find much that they agreed on when it came to sports or politics, but there was never any question about who was the best barber in Brooklyn: it had to be Mike, who operated a barber shop under the elevated New Lots IRT subway line on Livonia and Pennsylvania Avenues. The shop was located in a small storefront with a big glass window. The building looked like it hadn't been painted in the 75 or 100 years it had stood on the spot and the inside didn't look much different. Mike was a short, chubby guy who always needed a haircut himself and who was always in the middle of a pastrami or corned beef sandwich fresh from Ziggies Deli just a few stores away.

People from all over came to get their hair cut by Mike. The shop was a place where local guys hung out and passed time. When they walked through the doors of the shop, no one could be sure who was there to get a haircut and who came to just shoot the shit, until they heard Mike's familiar refrain, "Who next for a cut?"

There was only one problem with Mike. During Aqueduct race track season Mike would close at 1:30 pm in time to place his bet on the first race and reopen when he came back around 6pm. Sometimes, when he misjudged how long it would take to do a cut he would leave in the middle of the job and run out of the place to his car, announcing, "I gotta go." The unfortunate guy with half a haircut had a choice of sitting and waiting for Mike to return or putting on a hat and coming back after 6 p.m.

One day as my friend Marvin and I left the Biltmore poolroom and boxing gym, we decided to visit Mike's. Entering the store at about 2:30, we heard a bunch of guys breaking up with laughter. One of the guys was Joe Ancis sitting with half a haircut; the other guy was Jack Roy, aka Rodney Dangerfield. At the time, Joe and Rodney were partners in a home improvement business in Englewood, New Jersey.

As we walked in, Rodney was attempting to persuade Joe to put a hat over his half-done haircut and not miss his appointment to pitch the aluminum siding job scheduled for 4 o'clock. Joe kept saying he would call the customer, never referring to the customer as a "mooch," as did other shingle hustlers. Rodney and Joe were considered to be honest home improvement guys, not common at that time of kickbacks, inflated prices and jobs left unfinished after down payments were collected.

Rodney kept up a relentless harangue trying to persuade Joe to go "as is" because he felt the customer would cool off and the job would be lost to some other company. Joe kept arguing that the lead was solid and would not kick out. An ordinary business discussion turned to an argument as Joe began to berate Rodney with his inimical style of nasty satire and friendly jibes. As the two very funny guys went at each other, everyone in the shop couldn't stop laughing and were having a great time.

Finally Rodney left for New Jersey to do the pitch, but not before Joe told him if Rodney didn't secure the job, Joe would go back and tell the people the company was running a half-price sale in order to get the job. And he said he would make Rodney put the job up single-handed and place every sheet of aluminum as straight as his nose. Joe mimicked Rodney while standing in an upright position as if holding a sheet of siding, making funny faces and sounds. It was hilarious and ended with both partners leaving together. Joe was a funny guy. He has been credited with being Lenny Bruce's mentor and best friend, but Joe never set foot on a stage. I never found out if the job was sold, but it was one hilarious afternoon.

During that time, I stayed out late talking and smoking pot. I wasn't very good for work the next day and soon drifted into a deep depression, which was all too familiar to me. Eventually, after four years in the garment industry, I hung all my sexy samples of embroidered panties and bras in the Jubilee showroom and said goodbye, amid a sigh of relief to all concerned.

Chapter 14: Life's A Beach

Though I was again experiencing the old familiar insecure feelings, I knew I had to find some kind of work that paid the bills, and I tried to convince myself I was going to land something good. I guess I needed that illusion to keep me going. Since I had experience in the garment industry, I looked for a sales job, but had no luck. The future looked bleak.

One night my friend Bob and I were sitting in my old Ford listening to the famous Symphony Sid spin his jazz platters while sharing a couple of joints. Bob suggested we drive down to Florida. Since it was early December and the tourist season was starting, we felt we could get waiters jobs. I had never been to Florida, but it sounded like a good place to go.

We took off in my old Ford, driving straight through in about twenty hours. With the exception of a couple of flats that were easy to get repaired, the trip went pretty well, with one driving while the other slept. We ate grits with eggs when we stopped. I had always eaten potatoes with fried or scrambled eggs. Now here I was in South Carolina, half asleep, hearing the sweet voice of a pretty young waitress ask, "Y'all want grits with yer eggs?" What should have been a nice southern reply like, "yes ma'am," came out in our Brooklyn, "yeah, please."

When we got to South Miami Beach the sun was setting. The palm trees seemed to glow as they swayed with the breeze. I felt important. Here I was in a place I had heard only big shots came to vacation. At the first restaurant we entered, the people gave me the impression that they also felt as if they were in a special place. Like, "Hey look at me, I've made it now. Just me and my seersucker suit, and polyester floral pattern shirt."

After eating I wanted to take a walk on Collins Avenue, which I identified as the place to appear heading for some important venue. I soon discovered the South Beach Flagler Dog Track, a popular place to gamble and lose your money.

As we walked, Bob suggested a hotel he knew located right across from the ocean. The place appeared to me like a big old Southern colonial rooming house with a new paint job. It was cheap and clean. We took a room with twin beds and a shower in the hall for 18 bucks a night. I had about $200 in my pocket and Bob had about the same, so we took a couple of days to loaf around before looking for work.

I got up early and went across to the beach, noticing the palm trees that lined the sand. The sand was clean and almost white, like the sand on the Asbury Park Beach when I was a little kid. It sure had a Coney Island beat. The water was a rich, clear blue. From looking at it I thought it might feel different. When I started swimming, I soon found, as Shakespeare said, "All that glitters is not gold." The water was cold as hell.

When time came to start looking for work, Bob, having worked in Miami in the past, suggested a few places where he thought he knew the headwaiter. As it turned out, the places where he had worked had either changed management or had a different headwaiter, so we spent the rest of the day working on our sun tans back at the beach. It was much more crowded than it had been in the morning, with an added value. I noticed that the ladies were wearing new, mid-1950s European-style bathing suits, revealing much more in their curves. It didn't take me long to realize that bad eyesight was a disadvantage not just in boxing, but also on the Miami Beach shore line.

After an inexpensive supper we went back to the hotel, where we learned that a guy who had taken our number called and left a message saying we should get in touch with him. We called the next morning. He asked us to come to the Aladdin Hotel in the afternoon. Bob said he had worked there two years ago. It was an American Plan hotel, where the guests paid a flat rate by the week for their room and meals. He remembered that the hotel catered mostly to old folks. He also mentioned that he had done pretty well there. We made an appointment to see the headwaiter that afternoon.

When we got to the Aladdin we saw it was a big old antebellum structure with a beautifully decorated lobby and a small bar and piano in the front. We met Mel, the headwaiter who had called us. He told us that this was his second year as headwaiter at the Aladdin, and he mentioned some of the other places where he had worked. He asked us how much experience we had. Bob told him he had worked at the Aladdin four years ago. Mel asked Bob who the headwaiter had been, whereupon he and Bob got into a big discussion on the hotel industry. They both seemed to know what they were talking about. I got a few words in just to let Mel know I wasn't a complete novice.

Mel told us both to come in Sunday after lunch. A lot of seasonal guests would be arriving and he would give us both stations. He said, "Come in ready to work: white shirts, black pants, plain black shoes and black bow tie."

After leaving, Bob told me that when he had worked there before, most guests were elderly people who were well off and were good tippers or had well-healed kids who do the tipping for them. He said this was one of the last of the old time American Plan hotels that served Kosher food. I figured it would be similar to the Concord where I had worked several years back.

When we arrived ready to work on Sunday, Mel told us he would be having a meeting with his entire crew at 3 p.m. in the corner area of the dining room. An hour later we joined a group of about ten waiters and waitresses at the meeting. Mel greeted us all with a hearty hello. He introduced his regular crew, who had been working since September when the hotel reopened after the summer, to the new arrivals who he referred to as seasonal people.

He started by saying his name was Mr. Newman in front of customers, but "Mel" when talking to us, one on one. He said emphatically, "Service is our business and our guests come first. We never refuse anything. If there is ever a problem, you call me." And he added, "We don't get into conversations with outsiders on hotel business, whether it's Con Edison or the waiters' union."

He went on to talk about special diets, like salt free and low fat, and said we would be given a list of special foods required by some of the guests. He then delivered his punch line that got a good laugh, "This is no hospital. They're less concerned about special diets than we are. Any questions?" It was just like my waiter experience at the Concord, with the exception of the two words that would haunt me all winter: "special diet."

Mel then explained that Sam, the kitchen steward, would show all the new people around the kitchen and explain their system. After his orientation, Mel would assign stations and give us what he called "diet specs."

Sam's orientation was mostly about "working with your brain and not your feet." He stressed asking him if you needed help and ended with saying, "If you stay out of my way, I'll stay out of yours." It was a bit difficult for me to grasp, since, on the one hand, he wanted us to ask him for help, but, on the other hand, he wanted us to stay out of his way.

At the end of his orientation Sam wished us all the usual luck and said that was all he had for us. After Sam's talk I went up to Mel's desk. Mel handed me a paper with my assigned table numbers and the names of my guests. Those with dietary restrictions had a code by their name: N1 for No Sugar, N2 for No Salt, N3 for No Fat, an 's' after the number meant 'sometimes salt'. I thought it could be worse, out of sixteen guests at my tables, only half were on special diets.

I picked up the dinner menus from the headwaiter's desk and was glad to see that there were about three choices for each course, although the special diet restrictions were available for all the choices.

In American Plan dining, all livestock, like relishes, pickles, bread, and pitchers of water, are placed at the center of the tables, which seat about eight guests. The appetizers, called starters, are also placed at each setting before the guests arrive. At 6 p.m., the dining room opened and the guests began coming in, holding cards with their assigned table number. I joined the other waiters in helping guests find their assigned tables. When my two tables were about half full, I managed a smile and greeted them. "Hello, my name is Stan and I'll be your waiter." There were several seasoned replies: "Hello. I'm Mrs. Shapiro. You can call me Rose," and in a low voice, "I'm salt free." Or, "Hi, my name is Bernice and don't worry, we'll get along fine." "Hi we're Dave and Sarah Levy and you look like a nice boy. Booze with every meal." Dave was a joker who went to the racetrack most afternoons, often not getting back in time for dinner. All the diets were indicated on my guest list, but I guess the guests felt it didn't hurt to let me hear again.

As the guests were eating their appetizers, I took orders for the soup course. According to tradition, none of the waiters wrote the orders down, but trusted to memory. I got what was ordered correct, but didn't know who had ordered what. This irritated a few guests when I had to interrupt what seemed to be some interesting conversations. After the meal a few of my guests said things would get easier as we got to know each other better. A few mentioned that they would take good care of me and some even gave me part of the tip as front money. I smiled and thanked them.

It didn't take me long to find out that my memory wasn't good enough to work smoothly with all of the special diets. There was much more to focus on than just the choice of the item. There were several vegetable side orders that could be chosen with each entrée. A typical complaint might be, "Stendly, I ordered boiled beef salt free with regular string beans because I am allowed some salt, and salt free meshed potatoes." "Sorry Mrs. Rabinovitz, I'll exchange it for you." "Thenk you, dollink, your're so sveet."

After about three weeks of getting orders wrong and running back and forth to the kitchen making exchanges and getting on Sam's nerves, who told me I was "breaking his balls too much," I began to think the Aladdin wasn't for me. But I was making too much money to just quit. Every time I talked to Bob, who seemed to have no problems with the job, he said I was worrying too much. His favorite line was, "These old fucks don't know what they want to eat in the first place."

Sometimes I went to the dog track to bet on races. One night, I found myself standing on line to buy tickets for the next race with Dave Levy, the guest from the hotel. We both had bought losing tickets, so we started to talk after the race. Dave asked if I wanted to have a drink at the bar.

Dave was about 80 years old, very sharp, and a cool dresser. He always wore good polo shirts and neat light wool gabardine trousers with matching Florsheim shoes. He wore a high-end watch and a white gold star sapphire pinky ring. Pinky rings were big at the time. As we talked at the bar I made a few self-deprecating jokes about my waitering and we laughed. Saying he'd seen a lot worse, Dave asked me a lot of questions about my background. We talked for a long time.

After that, if we saw each other at the track, we always had a drink together. A few times we had a drink at B.S. Pully's Bar. B.S. Pully, the bar owner, was a friend of Dave's. He was also a standup comic who had starred in Guys and Dolls on Broadway. Dave told me that when B.S. is in town he always calls to hang out for a while

Dave told me a lot about himself, his two sons and the scrap metal business he owned in Cleveland, Ohio. His sons were now running the business. One son was very smart and the other guy he described as "a little slow."

I found that Dave liked to joke about the guests at the hotel. He told me Sunday night he was watching Jack Rabinovitz playing a poker game in the hotel card room. He said it looked to him like Jack was praying for good cards. The next morning at breakfast he asked Jack if he prays more in poker or in the Temple. Jack answered, "In the Temple, but in poker I really mean it."

When we drank, why I was waiting on tables came up. Although I wanted to change the subject, I told him I liked waiting on tables at the Aladdin. I said I would like to have more guests like him who didn't always show up for meals. His answer was, he used to stay further uptown in the upscale European Plan hotels, but he liked the Aladdin better because the residents were "real people."

The conversation took a more serious direction when I mentioned that while I also liked the people at the Aladdin, I was getting worn out with the special diets. I thought if I stayed there much longer the stress would add 50 years to my life and I would fit in perfectly. We both agreed that a change of venue for me would probably help.

I watched him thinking as we drank. Finally he looked at me and said, "I know this Union guy from my Jewish War Veterans Group. Go up and see him, you can tell him you know me." He said he had the address in his suite and that he would give it to me at breakfast in the morning.

After serving breakfast that morning I went to the address, bringing my old union book from when I helped organize at the Concord in the Catskills before going to the Army. A sign directed me up two flights of stairs to the Waiters and Bartenders Union. The office was well lit and clean. The first thing I noticed was a big, well-dressed guy standing behind a glass enclosure. A few people were working at desks around the office. The office had many chairs, but no one sitting in them, a sign of either no jobs or everyone working. I walked up to the glass enclosure, gave my name and mentioned that I was a friend of Dave Levy, which I don't think made much difference. All the guy behind the glass said was, "Dave Levy, nice person." I explained that I had been part of the organizing drive at the Concord in upstate New York and that I was now working at the Aladdin downtown, but wanted to change jobs.

The guy said his name was Al Cohen and that he was the business agent for the union. He asked if I had my union book. I showed it to him. He took a good look and asked how come I had never paid any dues. When I started to explain that I had been in the Army, he smiled and said he didn't have anything at the present time but I was welcome to sit and wait and maybe something would come in, or I could come back when I was ready to work.

He asked, "What's wrong with the Aladdin? You can make pretty good money there. You say you're an organizer. Maybe you can organize the place for us." I told him I was doing all right money-wise, but was having problems with the stress of special diets and the three-meal a day American Plan.

Loosening up, Al told me a little about Mel the head-waiter, saying, "That fat prick Mel is actually a union member and still pays dues. We've been trying to get him to bring the place in, but all he has are excuses." He asked if I had made any friends there. I mentioned my friend Bob Katz. Al asked, "If we start a drive to organize will you give us some help?" I said if I had another waiter's job, I would. When I told him I was going to leave the Aladdin after Sunday afternoon, he told me to come in when I was ready to work, he would try to do something for me.

After leaving the union office I took a quick drive along what was known as the Golden Mile along Collins Avenue. This was where all of the new upscale hotels that had recently been built were located. I stopped for a few minutes to look at the Eden Rock and the Fountainebleau. They were two hotels I had heard a lot about from the big shot guys who I had worked with when I was selling embroidery. They were very modern looking compared with the downtown art deco type buildings. I got a glimpse of the pool, which was huge with a lot of big umbrellas. These were the "class hotels" of the time, but later the South Beach Hotels came back strong and attracted the trendy hip crowd who had mega bucks to spend.

That night after dinner I told Mel that I had some per-

sonal trouble at home and had to go back to New York after finishing the week on Sunday. Mel asked when I could
come back and I said I would call him as soon as I knew. I
told the same story to the guests so they would be ready to
tip me on Sunday, which was always the weekly tip day.
Some asked me some questions about why I was leaving.
I felt like wisecracking that I got tired of walking in circles
returning dishes that were wrongly ordered, but I kept my
mouth shut. The tips were good on Sunday.

When I told Bob what was happening. All he said was,
"You might be better off."

I took a few days off and went to the beach uptown,
not wanting to be seen, but I really don't think anyone was
looking for me.

The following Wednesday morning I went up to the
union hall wearing the usual white shirt, black pants, bow
tie and black shoes. Al asked if I was ready to work and
told me to take a seat. After sitting for about an hour, Al
called me to the counter and asked if I wanted to work the
breakfast room at the Balmoral Hotel. He said the job was
7 a.m. to 4 p.m. On some days, I could also work dinner
in the main room. I knew the Balmoral as an upscale place
and took the job.

He gave me a paper with the address and who to see.
I met the headwaiter and, with no questions asked, he assigned me to a good station near the kitchen with two nice
windows and a view of the pool. The service was mainly
breakfast food, drinks and sandwiches. The prices were
higher than I had ever seen and the tips were good. I was
happy and had plenty of money to go to the South Beach
Dog Track and lose it.

As time went on I began to work in the main dining
room more, where the tips were even better. A waiter was
given four four-seat tables that usually filled up for din-

ner. Sometimes there was even a turnover, which gave me more people to serve. There was always a piano player who provided background music and sometimes sang. On weekends a show was presented after dinner, lending the room a nightclub atmosphere. Being new, the Balmoral was competing with the Fountainebleau and the Eden Rock – well- established hotels with clubs. The Balmoral booked some of the top performers at the time and attracted a crowd that had some money to spend. I got steady work in the club on Christmas and New Year's and on through January.

On Christmas Eve the hotel featured Roberta Sherwood, a top singer who, it was rumored, was having an affair with columnist Walter Winchell. We were full for two shows. She was so hot at the time that, on New Year's Eve, she packed the house again, and once more the waiters did well. Her singing was good. I enjoyed when I had time to listen and loved her rendition of "How Grand, How Nice." As Winchell said in his column, "Roberta Rocked the Room." A little publicity from Walter Winchell didn't hurt.

In the room that New Year's Eve was the notorious New Jersey Longshore boss, Willy Moretti, whose party included his elderly mother. The word was his tip was nowhere near the waiters' expectation.

I had a party from Texas of two well-dressed, bejeweled women and two guys wearing ten gallon Stetson hats. They ate and drank a lot, and I enjoyed serving them. When I presented the check one of the guys signed it with his name and room number. I brought it to the checker's desk. The waiter would get the tip amount that the party had written on the check. The checker at the desk said she couldn't read the amount of the tip and asked the captain of the section to straighten out the issue. I stood by and listened.

When the captain said that he could not read the tip amount, the tipsy guy slurred in his polite Texan way, "twen'y-faive cent." The captain laughed and I almost fainted thinking he was leaving me 25 cents. One of the ladies at the table cleared it up by explaining her husband meant twenty-five per cent, which was a great tip. I thanked Tex and company and gave him a free salute.

After we finished, one of the waitresses invited us to her house for a short party that I heard lasted until breakfast time. It was a great New Year's Eve.

About four days later while setting my station up, a guy came over and introduced himself as Hank Bueler. He said Al Cohen had told him I had some organizing experience and might be willing to help organize for the union. He asked me to meet him after work for a drink.

After work I met Hank at a 40-cent beer joint on Washington Ave. As we drank he explained that the Balmoral management and several other hotels on the Beach were fighting the Union and didn't want to recognize it. He asked if I would help organize. I said I would let him know during the week. I had seen Hank around but didn't know anything about him.

The next morning I called Al Cohen and told him about my meeting with Hank. Al said Hank is good and that I should work with him. He also said he would see to it that I got a stipend for my volunteer work and that I would be a big help to the organizing drive.

When Hank and I met the next day, he explained how the union was launching a big yearly organizing drive that would run through January and February. He said the union was asking waiters and waitresses to attend a brunch that was to take place soon. He gave me a list of people to speak with when I was at work. I was to read their nametag and invite workers known to be friendly to the union to the annual brunch.

Hank and I gave out leaflets each day at 10 a.m. in front of the area hotels that we were organizing. We looked mainly for people who were dressed in waiter's uniforms, asking them to call the number on the leaflet if they were interested. Every day, we hit a different hotel.

We usually worked for two or three hours and then went to lunch together, where I learned a lot about him. Hank's real first name was Hans. His family had gone from Germany to Canada and then to the United States in 1935. He described his family as having been anti-fascist activists, unable to live in Nazi Germany. He was told that one day, shortly after his family departed from Cologne, police came to their apartment in search of his father.

The only problem I encountered with Hank was the way he reacted to nasty people. He was usually polite, but if someone was disrespectful, he would tell them to "take a walk" or "fuck off," which is not correct for an organizer. A good organizer should never allow himself to be provoked. A few times we came so close to getting into physical altercations with company goons, that I started working out in the Fifth Street boxing gym for self-defense purposes.

Union benefits such as job security, health care and retirement were important organizing issues, but Al Cohen's brunch was always our major area of focus. While most people were receptive, I sensed fear in some we were talking with because the hotel owners did a thorough job of scaring folks into being against unions. I continued to work dinners at the Balmoral Hotel until the end of February and did pretty well.

I remember the afternoon that I stopped gambling. I was at the Gulf Stream Track with Dave Levy, my old friend from the Aladdin, and losing big time. I had $50 left in my pocket. My favorite jockey, Tony Desperito, was up on a horse named Go Forward. The betting board showed the odds at even money, meaning for every dollar wagered you get two back if your horse comes in first. I went to the $50 window and bet the last $50 I had in my pocket to win. If Go Forward won I would have collected $100, but the horse lost. I swore off gambling.

Luckily I had saved up about $2,000 and continued to work and to organize for the union. But February was a slow month. I was getting ready to go back home, though I wanted to wait for the Al Cohen brunch, which was scheduled on a Sunday morning at the end of the month. The place was packed and the food was plentiful: white fish, sturgeon, bacon, caviar, potato pancakes, omelets to order of all kinds, and even a glass of champagne. There were no speakers, just people walking around from room to room making small talk and collecting signed union cards. It looked like a success to me.

In March I hung out on the beach a lot. I got some banquet and convention work, but it was slow and I was getting ready to go back North. I had bought a 3 month membership at the Fifth Street boxing gym and was working out like a regular. The last two weeks in March was a real vacation for me. No work at all, just workouts at the gym, skipping rope for about 15 minutes and punching the heavy bag and the speed bag. After about 40 minutes I would look for someone to talk about the boxing business. I liked watching the big names spar. Many of the Champions, like Floyd Patterson, Mohammed Ali, Rocky Marciano and many more had trained at the Fifth Street Gym at one time or another.

I made friends with some of the boxers who worked out at the gym because I used to eat breakfast at a restaurant on Collins Avenue and Espanola Way, a hangout for boxers and boxing buffs where I could pick up some of the latest gossip in the boxing world. Stuff like which manager is able to get the best matches for their boxers, who the best trainers were, and which fighters were willing to throw a bout. Stuff nobody needs to know.

I sparred a few times with my friend, Mickey Crawford. He was a welterweight, probably about 25 pounds lighter than me. What he gave up in weight he gained in speed. It was hard for me to see where the punches were coming from and they came fast. I wore head gear and body protection. It was an experience, but no fun. All I ever learned from the few times I sparred was that I wasn't much of a fighter. After hanging out in the gym I would have lunch and hit the beach for some sun and water. I even met a few women and had a couple of dates during my last two weeks in Florida. It was a good season.

Whenever I got together with my friend Bob he seemed tired. I'd seen him only a few times during the season. He was still at the Aladdin and I asked how Mel was treating him. He said a lot of the guests Mel was giving him were very old people whose kids did the tipping and the gratuity charges were just added to the bill. He asked when I was going back to New York. I told him in March and he asked if I could wait until the end of the month. I agreed to and we went back together in my car.

I made all my after-season good byes at the end of March. Al asked me to stay. He said he could give me work in the off season, but my mind was made up. I didn't like waiting tables. After splurging on four new tires for the Ford, Bob and I decided to drive back to the city on the last weekend. I even made sure my bank account had a New

York branch. I said good-bye to Miami Beach and headed home, with no idea what in the hell I was going to do next.

.

Chapter 15: A cabbie In The Big Apple

On the drive back from Florida with Bob I tried to have a serious discussion about where we were headed in life. It was a little hard to keep him focused on the issue because all he ever seemed to want to do was get laid, smoke pot, and bet on baseball games. He did speak about opening a restaurant, but said that he had to put together a lot more money than he had. As a reformed gambling addict I didn't mean to be harsh, but I mentioned that I didn't think he was going to do it by betting baseball, because the bookies had an edge and the odds were in their favor. He asked me why I didn't stick with selling. When I told him I wasn't good at it he said I didn't give myself enough of a chance and became discouraged too fast, the same observations other people had made to me.

The fact was, selling and waiting tables felt like dead-end jobs. I felt like a failure in them and knew I had to look for something else.

Bob mentioned that he had been a cab driver before becoming a waiter, and that a person could make money driving a cab. He had been suspended for riding stick up, so during the suspension he took a waiting job. Laughing as he spoke, he said, "That's how I got to be a waiter. I liked waiting better and never went back to driving."

Ashamed to ask what riding stick up meant, I didn't find out until a few months later. It simply meant negotiating a flat rate with the customer and not pushing the lever down to put the meter on. That meant the driver keeps the whole amount for the ride, keeping the cab company from getting its percent. I never got into riding stickup because it was a serious offense that could lose you your license. Some drivers still did it.

Having saved up some money while working on the Beach, I thought of going to one of the trade schools, since I had some schooling coming to me as a recipient of the GI Bill. I investigated auto mechanics, but didn't really have a feel for it. Carpet installation and repair sounded good, so I checked it out. Nothing seemed to be working for me.

Remembering my talk with Bob, I answered an ad in the Daily News for cabdrivers and was given a short interview by one of the garage owners. The owner gave me a letter of sponsorship to go down town to the taxi commission the next morning and apply for a taxi operator's license. The taxi commission was located in a large building on a high floor in the Wall Street area. When I got to the floor, I noticed a sign that directed me to a large area with many chairs. A smiling gent with a neat blue suit and bow tie showed me a seat. As I sat down, he handed me an application, explaining what sections to fill out and where to bring the application when I finished it. When I brought it to the appropriate desk, a tall, well-dressed woman thanked me, placed it in a stack of applications and asked me to have a seat.

After about 40 minutes my name was called and I was told to go behind a curtain, where I was asked to strip to the waist. Next my blood pressure and heart were checked. Then I was directed to another room where a big guy with a white coat stood behind me and in a low voice said repeat after me, as he mentioned some streets and questions about directions which he asked me to answer. I think this was a combination geography and hearing test, which I seemed to pass.

Next I was asked to read an eye chart by another guy

in a white coat. When I got down to the last line, I think I missed a few letters because his last statement to me was, "I'm going to pass you." As I walked out of the room, the guy who gave me the eye test gave me a thorough look. I think he wanted to remember me and I could never figure out why. Maybe he wanted to avoid taking my cab at all costs for his personal safety.

The last part of the process was the orientation, which was given by an old time New York cabby. He talked about safety and politeness being our most important considerations. He told us to read the book on rules and regulations that we had been given. The last part of the day was his anecdotal assessment of New York cabbies, which went like, "Now, our cabbies are dressed neatly and usually wear a nice hat and, sometimes, even a necktie. And one thing that everybody knows about them is that they know everything. So naturally, the passengers are going to ask you a lot of questions and you'll know the answer to most of them. But don't be afraid to say you don't know, if you don't know the answer, because believe me, this will be refreshing to a lot of people, including native New Yorkers, and will make you a novel character in this great city of ours. So, good luck to you one and all."

I hadn't been through anything like this since my Army induction exam and was excited about the prospects of my new endeavor as a cab driver. I remembered some older guys who hung out on one of the street corners in Brooklyn where a taxi stand was located. They lined their cabs up three or four at a time and waited for riders. When the front cab got a passenger they moved up. Sometimes I would listen to their conversations about this fare and that airport job or a hotel that was good to get riders at, or what nightclub was good to work when they pulled the night tour. I got the impression they did pretty well and was looking forward to getting started.

When I got my license I was placed on the day line working the 8 am to 4 pm shift. Working Manhattan was not bad and, as the guy at the orientation said, I did get asked a lot of questions, like, "Cabbie, what's the best department store in town?" or, "Where can I buy a really good guitar for cheap?" or, "Hey, Cabbie, you know any joints where a guy could get laid?" At first, I really tried hard to give good answers, but soon found that it lead to too much bullshit and was distractive, so I just gave my standard answer like, "Sorry sir, sorry m'am, but I don't know."

I liked listening to the conversations of the passengers. There was one hot summer afternoon when two guys in nice double-breasted blue suits with a bunch of sharp accessories hailed me on 8th Avenue somewhere in the 40s. They placed a lot of equipment in the trunk of my cab. They were both sweating and looked kind of exhausted, as if they were having a very tough day.

I asked, "Where to?" One of the guys said Luchow's Restaurant on 14th Street and the other guy says Tavern on the Green in Central Park. I stopped near a fire hydrant and just listened to those two men have a friendly argument on where to go, while watching that no cops were coming in my direction to give me a ticket. One of the men argued that he had eaten in Luchow's "twice already this week" and the other guy said he, "didn't want to lug the bags into Central Park in all this heat". Getting anxious that I might get an expensive parking ticket, I stated in no uncertain terms that I was not interested in getting a "fucking $100 parking fine." One of the guys laughed and said, "The Sacred Cow on 72nd Street." As I headed north, the real business discussion started; they began discussing trading film footage from their porno flicks. The first guy said he still wasn't willing to give up the footage of the blow job scene in the dentist's office in his film "Drilling in the Suburbs". The second guy said he would give up the footage of the fuck scene in his masterpiece film "Behind the Behind" as a trade for the Blow Job Scene that he wanted and sweeten the deal by throwing in the Orgy scene in "Clergy Picnic" as a bonus to clinch the deal. As we arrived at the destination I noticed both guys in deep thought in my rear view mirror. In all the haggling, both guys walked into the restaurant without asking for the stuff they had put in the trunk, which I also didn't remember until I had driven a full city block on 72nd Street. I made a quick U-turn and went back to the restaurant. I took the bags full of video equipment into the restaurant to where the guys were sitting. After a barrage of "thank you, thank you, thank you," one of the guys handed me a twenty dollar bill. The other guy asked how much his friend had given me. I showed him the twenty dollar bill. He said, "Cheap fuck" and handed me twenty more. Not being a porno enthusiast, I never found out how or if the deal was consummated. I was happy with the $40.

A few times I worked the night shift where there was a lot more action, dealing with drunks, hookers, junkies and some nice working folks. I might have stuck with the night shift, but I found that my nearsightedness got in the way of seeing streets and building numbers, so I stayed on days.

Working Manhattan was alright, but when I got jobs out in the boroughs, I usually got lost and wasn't much good at map reading. I thought driving a cab would be interesting, and on some days it was, but I soon found out that looking at the rear bumpers of cars and being stuck in traffic was more than I wanted to handle. The garage I worked out of, Ding a Ling, was located on Charles and

Hudson Streets in Greenwich Village and did have some interesting characters driving at the time. With the recent economic recession, we had some very educated men and ladies pushing hacks, including Oliver Stone, who drove a cab while attending NYU film school.

Taking up half a city block, the garage appeared like a fortress, with unpainted stucco walls. There were some old Checker cabs, but mostly newer Dodge and Plymouth cabs parked from wall to wall. The smell of carbon exhaust and dry heat was always present. In one of the corners were a set of benches and the enclosed office of the dispatcher who assigned cabs to drivers at the beginning of each shift. In this area many interesting discussions took place. The main topic was the war in Vietnam, which most of the drivers felt we should not be involved in. Some disagreed vigorously, usually the older drivers, who were more conservative. They argued in favor of "stopping communism before it came to our country." Yeah, right. A few were Korean War era veterans like myself, who had mixed feelings about our involvement in what we referred to as an illegal, immoral and unjust war being fought for the control of tin, tungsten and rubber.

We were all members of the recently organized taxi drivers union Local 3036 under the leadership of Harry Van Arsdale, Jr., a leader of the Central Labor Council of New York. Most of the drivers liked the new union, called Taxi Drivers United, but some believed only a union where the officials were working drivers and not union bureaucrats would win better conditions for drivers.

Several drivers bought this argument, which sounded solid in theory, and formed a group called "Taxi Rank and File." I sometime attended the meetings held every Wednesday in an old church on West 28th Street, where I learned a lot about union history and the cab industry.

Some members were in left political parties, but most were just dissatisfied with the current recession and conditions in general and wanted to participate in something they thought would bring about social change.

After meeting for about two years, the group decided to run a candidate against President Van Arsdale. Our candidate was Leo Lazerus, a man who had been driving for many years and had a reputation for being an honest, dedicated supporter of working people. I didn't think he had much of a chance against Van Arsdale, but since I had thrown my lot in with the rank and file group and made friends with some great people, I campaigned for Leo.

Given the limited resources we had and the powerful machine we opposed, we did surprisingly well, garnering 37% of the vote. After the election we continued to meet and discuss why we lost and how we could do better in the next election. One of the members was a Brooklyn guy who had been driving for a long time and always talked about organizing a "collision," which I eventually understood meant a "coalition."

Though the discussions were usually friendly and respectful, on one occasion a fist fight took place which was broken up before anyone got hurt. The subject of women's rights was always a hot topic. Charlie and Joyce were partners and both had degrees in chemistry. They had two small children and often got into arguments about what the role of each should be in their domestic chores. We all looked forward to these arguments because they were very funny.

A few times the drivers had softball games on Sunday afternoons. One time a big argument occurred because Charlie and Joyce both wanted to pitch, but they were on the same team. When Joyce finally agreed to play the outfield, Charlie jokingly protested, saying he wanted to play the outfield, too.

Then there was Eve, who had a degree in speech ther-apy from a French Canadian university and could not get a job in her chosen field. Someone suggested that she couldn't get a job in her field because English was not her first language. She got very pissed off at the guy and said, "You don't know what the fuck you're talking about" in perfect English.

The baseball games continued long after most of us went into other jobs. A yearly reunion game in Brooklyn's Prospect Park provided some great laughs for all. I've heard Joyce and Charlie are still fighting about the same issues, only now it's in reference to their grandchildren.

After about eight months of driving, not making much money and being lost on the road half the time, I decid-ed driving a cab wasn't for me. Thoughts about my par-ents' relationship began coming into my mind more often around this time. I needed time to think things over, so I parked my cab and set off on foot, searching for answers without really knowing what the questions were.

.

Chapter 16: Village Life

The year was 1968. I was living in Manhattan in an inexpensive East Village apartment on 12th Street and Avenue A and spending a lot of time just sitting in Union Square Park, which was about all I wanted to do at the time. I thought I was having some kind of breakdown, with memories of my childhood and the yelling and cursing filling my waking day dreams. I considered asking one of my brothers or my father for financial help, but I hadn't seen them since the breakup of my first marriage three years before and couldn't bring myself to ask. It would be like admitting defeat.

For several months I had been thinking more about the death of my mother. The feelings really got me down when I was driving a cab. I thought I would feel better if I took it easy for a while, but I was wrong. Not knowing for sure how she died fed my frustration, and my anger became much worse. Often I sat and just gritted my teeth. At times, I could see my father doing something terrible to my mother on the last day of her life. I was beginning to lose interest in many of the things that once were important to me.

One of my friends suggested that I go to the Veterans Hospital and speak with a therapist, which I did. I was given a one hour appointment with a middle aged, female therapist. I told her about myself and what I was thinking about my mother's death. I talked about my background and my marriage to my first wife. I remember her asking what I considered the three most important things I wanted in life. I said women, an end to war, and money. It was a relief having someone to talk to.

The therapist prescribed some anti-depressant medication, explaining it would calm me down. I was given an appointment to return in a week. The first question the therapist asked during my second appointment was whether I was taking my medication. When I answered that I had taken some of the pills, but not on the regular schedule that was prescribed, she asked why? I explained that the medication made me tired and I just wanted to sleep after taking it. She asked me to try taking a nap each day, it might make me feel better, and gave me another appointment to come back.

After about six weeks, both the therapist and I came to the conclusion I should try to do without medication and continue to see her twice a month. Although I was feeling a little better, the anger was still there.

I continued to see her for six months, mainly because I did like talking with her. In time we both realized that what I needed to feel better was to start making some money. The insecurity and the poverty may have been to some degree self-imposed, but the depression was for real. The war in Vietnam was raging and it was hard to turn a corner without seeing some kind of protest in motion. I was beginning to see some aspects of my own life more clearly.

While working two jobs, I met a woman, Sheila, in 1965 and married her after a short time. Though we got along fine, I found myself always getting into arguments with her parents. It became apparent that I had acquired not only a wife but also an overbearing mother-in-law and an aggressive father-in-law.

After being married for only eleven months, she wanted me to get a third job. When I refused, she sued for annulment on the grounds that I was lazy. The marriage lasted long enough for Sheila to empty our bank account of the $3,000 we had saved together. She said the account was hers, because she got to the bank before I did. I didn't have the energy to deny her logic.

Since being discharged from the Army in 1956, I had had many jobs. I had worked in garment sales, telemarketing, encyclopedia sales, sold home improvements and, on weekends, worked as a waiter at the Diamond Club in the Shea Stadium dining room. I really don't know why I always wanted to do sales jobs, I never liked having to sell in the first place. I thought that if the product was good, it would sell itself. I didn't learn that this was a formula for failure until I had bounced around a smorgasbord of jobs. Though not a very good salesman, I knew people who were successful at selling and made a lot of money, and I believed I could do the same. I was told that I should be more aggressive and smile more – a really hard task for me.

Luckily, I was able to keep a roof over my head by always going back to waiting on tables. Though I swore off waiting on tables a hundred times, I still held on to my union book from the Concord Hotel. I would shape up as an extra at the union hiring hall and be sent to banquet jobs in hotels on a rotation basis. I liked being able to make enough as a part-timer on weekends to carry me through the week.

When Jack Shimmel, the labor chief in charge of job placement and one of the original organizers of the waiters union, learned that I had been part of an organizing effort in the Catskills and in Florida, he asked me to help out with some organizing work for the union during the week. Sometimes I would be given locations to go leaflet and talk to the workers about the benefits of being a union member. The organizing activity was rewarding and meant some additional money.

I was still spending much of my spare time in Union Square Park in Manhattan. Famous for the labor demonstrations that had taken place there for a hundred years, the park had a rich history of working class orators holding forth on capitalism and the class struggle: in other words, getting screwed by the boss.

One day a guy told me about a group being formed by military veterans who were against our involvement in the war in Vietnam. I attended the first meeting and was impressed by the caliber of men and women present. Unlike myself, who had served after the Korean conflict was over, many of these folks were heroes of World War II. Some had seen action in Korea. There were even veterans of the Abraham Lincoln Brigade who had fought in the Spanish Civil War of 1936 against General Franco's fascists, who had taken over the Spanish Republic with help from Hitler and Mussolini.

At that first meeting, we voted to join a larger group, the Fifth Avenue Parade Committee to participate in a peace parade that was to take place two weeks later on 5th Avenue. When the planning committee for the parade heard of our newly formed group, we were chosen to march at the head. I was proud to be marching with the vets, many of whom wore their medals. The parade was a huge success, with many thousands in attendance and many more cheering from the sidelines.

Since I have always had great difficulty keeping my ideas to myself, I began to get into discussions on the job with my co-workers. I was surprised to learn that, with few exceptions, most of the people I talked with supported the war in the early years of our involvement. This changed as the U.S. escalated the war and people began to learn more about what was happening, like the use of napalm to kill Vietnamese people and Agent Orange to defoliate the Vietnamese countryside, not to mention the terrible toll taken by our young men and women in combat. The American people slowly began to realize that this was about "tin, tungsten and rubber."

Emotions ran high in our talks. At times heated arguments occurred. I remember a couple of times getting into debates with paying customers at banquets or in restaurants. Adding insult to injury, the union leadership did not support the anti-war movement. They began giving me fewer jobs at farther away destinations. Even my organizing work was cut. At times, I had to allow two hours for travelling by bus one way to a banquet hall out on Long Island. It occurred to me that if I was going to spend this much time on the bus, maybe I should take the test for bus driver.

I spent most of my spare time participating in the sexual revolution and arguing for a political revolution. My lifestyle did not require nearly as much money for living expenses as when I was married, but I was fast running out of the small stash I had managed to put away.

Around this time I became a bit more outgoing and better able to socialize. I developed a more spiritual outlook on life and was convinced I was doing something worthwhile with my anti-war activities. I also took in some cultural events. One Sunday afternoon after a lecture at NYU on cave man art, I saw a beautiful woman sitting on a couch in the school lobby. Her name was Betty. I felt a strong attraction to her. After dating for about a month we moved in together. I thought I was in love for the first time in my life and wanted to marry her. But I really needed a way to make a living, and the old familiar feeling of desperation had come back to haunt me.

I discussed this with a new friend, Ken Doolittle, whom I had met in Union Square Park. Ken was a bit older than myself and worked as an elevator operator at Mount Sanai Hospital in Manhattan. He had three children in college and loved to prove he knew more than they were learning.

In the 1930s Ken was the live-in lover of the now-famous portrait artist, Alice Neel. When Alice dumped him for an affluent doctor, he asked her what he should do now. She told him to go to Spain and fight the Fascists. He did go to Spain and fought heroically, but not before slicing up all of her finished paintings, leaving only one painting intact: a portrait of him donned in one of his flamboyant outfits.

Decades later, around 1966, Ken and I ran into Alice at the Symphony Space Theatre on Broadway and 96th Street. Communist Party leader Gus Hall was speaking about a world tour he had just made. Ken said hello to her and introduced me as his friend. She invited us up to her apartment after the talk. That night as the two former lovers reunited, I liked to listen to them reminiscing about the radical movement of the 1930s and all the characters they met back in the day. It was an evening I will never forget.

Ken was never short of ideas and not shy about giving advice. He told me about his career as a merchant seaman before going to Spain. After his stint in the Spanish Civil War he was unable to get work as a seaman because he had participated as a member of the Abraham Lincoln Brigade. Our government labeled all of the people who took part as communists.

As a result of this blacklisting, Ken bought an old truck, equipped it with a coffee urn and drove around to various work-sites selling coffee, cake and sandwiches. When I asked him whether he made much money he answered, "more than enough and more than I ever made before," adding that vending was a good business in the city and that I might give it a try.

When I walked in the crowded business districts I had never given much thought to the street vendors I saw peddling their wares. That evening as I was walking home, I saw two guys selling the same item on a busy corner. They seemed to be embroiled in an argument and about to get into a fistfight. Using this as a pretext to get some information, but also not wanting the guys to fight, I walked up and asked what the problem was. One of the guys blurted out that "this motherfucker had stolen his item," which I later found out meant selling the same item as another peddler at the same location. I took careful notice of the item. It was a glass ball with a battery that lit up a Christmas scene of the birth of Jesus with falling snow. It was quite impressive and felt like a sure thing to sell, this being early December. I asked where I could purchase this item wholesale, not expecting a serious answer. To my surprise, one of the men blurted out in heated anger, "You wanna be a peddler? Go to Benny's Novelty on Broadway and 17th Street!"

This was how I began my career as a street peddler.

Chapter 17: Street Peddling

The morning after I met the battling street venders, I went to Benny's Novelty Store and spotted the item I was interested in. There were twelve dozen balls in a box divided into three four-dozen parts, which included the Nativity, Crucifixion, and Resurrection scenes. The price was $6 a dozen wholesale; $.50 for each piece. The street selling price was one dollar a piece. I purchased two boxes to try my luck.

That afternoon I began to sell in front of the Armory on 7th Avenue and 14th Street. I was doing all right for about an hour when a cop came over and asked for my vendor's license. When I told him that I had none and didn't know that I needed one, he issued me two summonses, one for no license and the other for peddling in a restricted area. He ordered me to pack up my merchandise and leave. I took a fast inventory and noticed that I had sold three and a half boxes, which netted me about twenty one dollars profit, less what I would have to pay for the summonses. Not wanting a confrontation so early in my new career, I packed up, put the stuff in the trunk of my 1960 English Ford Zodiac that I had recently purchased for 100 bucks and drove off, planning what my next move would be.

As I drove east on 14th Street, I noticed the peddler who told me where to buy the item. I parked at a meter, walked up to him, and introduced myself. His name was Eddie. When I told him I had bought the item on his recommendation, he almost fainted. Apparently, he didn't think I would take him seriously. I asked him as one peddler to another if we could have coffee when he finished work. He said I should come back after "the blow-off." I was too embarrassed to ask what "the blow-off" was. But he read the blank look on my face and said it was when the store that he was working in front of closes. That was Mays Department Store on Broadway and 14th Street, one of the largest department stores in the City, with people coming and going all day.

I came back about twenty minutes before closing time. Three minutes before the doors closed, an outpouring of shoppers converged on his display, three glass balls on top of a high box. The last-minute shoppers bought with a passion. My friend could not pass out the glass balls fast enough, even with me helping. He sold almost every piece he had.

Eddie was in a great mood as we went to Horn and Hardart on 14th Street for coffee. Horn and Hardart was one of the last of the old style cafeterias where food was secured by inserting money in slots in front of desired dishes displayed behind glass windows. The window would open and the food could be removed. Workers behind the large glass encasements would then replace the dishes that had been purchased.

As soon as we entered the restaurant, some of the guys sitting at tables, engrossed in animated conversations, smoking, and drinking coffee, looked up and greeted my new friend, Eddie the Peddler. We both bought sandwiches and coffee and sat down at one of the tables. Eddie seemed curious about what my interests were and why I was turning to street peddling. When I talked a bit about what was happening in my life, I saw that Eddie understood. As our entrepreneurial attitudes began to mesh, the conversation took a philosophical turn. I found myself listening to a dialectical analysis of how profit is derived from the marketing and handling of a commodity rather than its true value. He sounded like a cross between Jack London and Lloyds of London. It was as if a Chaplanesque character was being molded before my eyes. His long coat and shabby oversized suit, with big black shoes, added an air of drama to his presence.

When Eddie found out that I had an honorable discharge from the Army, he advised me to go to the City Clerk's office and obtain a peddling license. He explained that I would still get summonses, but if I worked properly, the small fines imposed could be considered part of operating expenses. He talked about being in a position to buy the same product as the retail store owner, but at a better price, because he paid cash, a strong advantage with a supplier who always loves cash customers. He filled me in on the tremendous advantage of being able to move around and set up where the action was. Going directly to the source to buy was also an advantage, because it's always better to see what you are getting than to receive a trucked-in shipment. This guy should have been a motivational speaker.

He did give me the downside, explaining that the peddler is always in violation of some municipal statute or regulation no matter where they go, and that most cops would always find a reason to give a ticket. But these were just operational nuisances which were overcome by not having to pay the huge rents that retail operations faced.

After a long talk we got up and said goodbye to each other. As I was leaving, I saw him walk back over to where the regulars were seated. The automat was a hangout for all kinds of colorful characters. Eddie was no exception. In the future his name would come up often in the grapevine of Lower East Side characters.

The next morning, I was first on line at the City Clerk's

office with my Army discharge in hand. The clerk told me the price of the license was one dollar. I had been expecting some red tape and maybe a waiting period, but was pleasantly surprised at the immediate issuance of a neat 8"x10" calligraphied license affirming my right to peddle, vend, hawk, and solicit business in any non-restricted area within the confines of New York City. I went home to pick up my car and drove to the wholesaler, where I purchased as many cases as my car could hold. I then went back to my apartment and unloaded all but three cases. At this time, I did not know many "spots," so I went to the spot I had first seen Eddie working

It was late afternoon. I parked my car at a meter, opened one of my boxes and made a crude display of my item. At first, business was slow. I had second thoughts about my new venture and began to think that maybe the other guys had saturated the spot. Before the fear of failure could take hold, the street became very busy with shoppers coming from every direction. As it was three weeks before Christmas, I was sure that many people considered this a fine gift for a friend or family member. In any event, I began to sell at a frenetic pace. At one point, a policeman came over and asked me for my license. I presented him with my brand new document. He examined it and told me that the area was restricted to peddling, but that he would not give me a ticket this time. Being around the same age and seeing my veteran's license, I think he felt some compassion.

I continued to sell like hotcakes. Thinking it was important to maintain the tempo of the sales, I broke into a chant as people pointed to the glass ball they wanted to purchase. I would shout with the cadence of a preacher, "A Nativity for the gentleman," or "The lady would like a Last Supper." Or maybe "A Resurrection for the young man!" As I looked into the eyes of the people, some looked as if they were experiencing a religious event. One man even crossed himself and then touched my heart. I returned a warm and sincere smile and felt a genuine affinity to these people who were buying my product.

After all, Jesus was considered to be the Prince of Peace, and wasn't I a peace activist? I began to have illusions of being a latter day secular disciple as I approached selling out my three boxes by five o'clock. As my adrenaline began to come back to its normal level, I realized that I should have brought more boxes with me, but I still had a good day.

I drove home to the Lower East Side where Betty and I were living in a one room apartment, anxious to tell her of my adventure. As soon as I got into the house I began an animated talking spree. After counting the proceeds, which were correct, give or take a dollar or two, we celebrated our first successful business day with a Chinese dinner at Hung Fat, my favorite storefront restaurant on Catherine Street in Chinatown.

The next day was Saturday. I got off to a good start bright and early with the remaining nine boxes of glass balls. I parked my car and unloaded three cases, leaving five cases in the trunk, which was all it could hold, and one case on the back seat. I proceeded to what I now considered was my corner on 14th Street with three cases on a small dolly. As I approached the corner I discovered a man I had never seen before selling flowers. I walked up to him and told him that I had been working the corner and that it was my corner. He was a much older man than myself, dressed in a worn overcoat and fedora hat, with an old necktie and shirt. His face bore several scars, including an old wound running from his eyebrow down across his eye to his cheek.

In a low, deliberate tone he told me that he didn't much

give a fuck who I was, that 14th Street was an open street, and that anybody could work any corner they wanted. He asked if I had a car. When I said yes and pointed across the street to my car, he said I could make good money with this item at 149th Street and 3rd Ave in the Bronx.

I knew a little about the Bronx neighborhood from my cabbie days. Since a high percentage of my customers from the day before had been Puerto Rican, I figured it was worth a try and went up to the Bronx. When I got to the spot, I parked on a side street and again unloaded three cases, leaving five in the trunk and one on the back seat. I wheeled my three cases around the corner, not sure exactly where I was. But I did see a lot of people. As I opened my boxes, I noticed that I was about thirty feet away from the front entrance to Alexander's Department Store.

After I displayed my item a security guard from the store came out and politely told me that I was too close to the store entrance. I knew that he did not have the final say on this matter, since I was outside of the store, but his massive build and confident demeanor persuaded me to move. He pointed to a fire hydrant just a little back from where I was standing, saying that in front of the hydrant was a good spot. I asked his name and shook hands with him as I moved to the fire hydrant.

After arranging my merchandise, I began a slow deliberate chant as I had the day before on 14th Street. Business was slow at first, probably because it was only about 11 o'clock. Before I could even look at my watch again, it was 12:30 and I had sold out the three cases I had brought from the car. I raced back around the corner to my car, feeling good about getting off to such a good start. As I approached the car, key in hand, I noticed a broken window. My first thought was that I had been ripped off, but for a split second I was hoping against the odds that my stock would still be there. So much for hope. I had been cleaned out, trunk lock broken and all.

While driving home in that early afternoon, I knew I had just been taken. I thought about getting more of my item, but first had to deal with the security problem. I tried to avoid any self-pity because I did not want to become depressed and take a defeatist attitude. I thought for a moment that the guard from the store might have been behind what had happened, but I had sized him up as a decent guy and considered myself a good judge of people.

In any event, I was convinced that the basic premise of the peddling business was correct for me at this time in my life and I wasn't going to let a little setback stop me. I drove to a window repair shop where the service was good and fast. I asked the window repair guy if he could fix my trunk lock and he sent me to a place where they could do something so I could lock the trunk. I wound up with a clasp that I could put a big padlock on that worked okay.

I still had enough time to go to Benny's and buy twelve more boxes of merchandise. When he brought the boxes up from the basement storage, I reached into my pocket and discovered that I was $35 short of what I needed. I asked if he would trust me until tomorrow and he said it was against company policy. I thought of trying to convince him to trust me, but his cold stare told me that he was not a very trusting soul. I went home and got the money, making sure to unload the car.

Since the time was early evening and Betty was not home, I thought about going out to work the night rush. The "blow off". My better judgment told me to take a break, I already had done a full day's work. Though anxious to not lose my selling momentum, I reminded myself that the sidewalk would still be there the next day. I left the house to find a place to eat, able to afford a decent supper even with my unexpected expenses.

As I walked down around 14th Street, I saw a guy selling ladies hats at a pace as fast as I had been selling the glass balls. This man had a handsome, weather-beaten face. The hats were hood-like garments made of imitation fur, with two strings and a little ball at the end of each string to tie into a bow. He was charging three bucks a piece and I figured his rate of profit was about a third. From across the street I clocked him for 15 minutes and recorded 30 sales at a time that was not even the busy time of the evening. Making a mental note of his sales success, I went into Horn and Hardart.

After purchasing a piece of fish and a couple of vegetables, I sat at an empty table and ate my meal. I noticed Vincent, the peddler I had the beef with on 14th Street who had sent me to the Bronx, sitting with a couple of guys from the Union Square Park lecture set. One of these men, called Dr. Moe, was a black man with a husky build and large, intelligent eyes. He spoke like a Southern Baptist preacher and always made comical references to the people who worked in the nearby office buildings, who he said liked to get dressed up and play the part of millionaires but couldn't even afford a baloney sandwich for lunch. He talked of the nearby dilapidated tenement flats with their rats as big as cats playing football with each other. He also had some choice words for the rent-gouging landlords whose railroad flats, he said, "Had more violations than Jesse James in his heyday." He liked to refer to doctors as Masters of Science Fiction. Everyone got a big kick out of Dr. Moe. He was in the true tradition of the street philosopher.

The other man at the table was Sidney Von Luther, a fellow who also soap-boxed in the park. He was short and round, spoke with an erudite West Indian accent, and had a few choice words about the system of Capitalism that weren't complimentary. I got to know Sidney as time went on. He was employed by the Drug and Hospital Workers Union as an organizer when I first met him and went on to become a New York State Senator.

After finishing my food, I got a cup of coffee and went up to the table where these guys were seated. I greeted Vincent, who motioned for me to sit down. Although I had not formally met the two men sitting with Vincent, we had seen one another often in Union Square when I was hanging out. We talked about the temporary employment agencies that supplied the restaurant workers, mainly dishwashers and kitchen help. Dr. Moe tore into these organizations, which he referred to as slave labor pimps. Sidney spoke of the need for these workers to be organized into a decent union. I enjoyed listening, since I had been a waiter for years and was familiar with the industry.

After about 15 minutes Vincent asked me how I had done that day. I told him about my stock being stolen up in the Bronx. With a deadpan look on his face he said that I should never have locked the car, since it probably would have been broken into anyway with my merchandise in clear view. At least I would have saved the window repair. One of the other guys added that I should have hung around to see who did it and maybe I could have bought my goods back. We all had a good laugh at my expense.

When Vincent saw that I was embarrassed, he said that at least I didn't get discouraged, since I'd gone right out and bought more goods to sell – a remark I took as a compliment, and felt a lot better. As the conversation turned to peddling, the other two men at the table seemed to become less interested and began talking to each other. I thanked Vincent for telling me about the spot in the Bronx, because

I was doing real well until I discovered the thieves who emptied my car had done better. Vincent told me that the glass balls were a pretty hot novelty item before Christmas and that there would probably be a lot of competition for the next ten days or so.

I told him about the guy I'd seen selling the hats. Vincent knew Al and filled me in on him. He laughed as he described how selfish and petty the man could be.

Vincent told me about how Al had been a driver with one of the big trucking companies in town, but had gotten into trouble over some goods that disappeared off a truck he'd been driving. Vincent even told me that he and several other people he knew had bought goods from Al not knowing where they came from. I began to get nervous, because I had learned as a kid that it wasn't good to know too much of other people's business. I even wondered why Vincent was sharing all this information with me, but figured that he was just a guy who liked to talk and kind of trusted me.

A little later, when it was just the two of us at the table, Vincent asked where I got the idea to start street peddling. He asked where I lived and if I was married and had any children. I told him about my woman friend and that we were going to have a child soon. He asked whether we were planning marriage. I had to explain that my woman was still married and that her divorce was in the process. I asked if he was married and he abruptly said, "long ago and far away." We talked for a little longer; shook hands and parted company.

On my way home I thought about how I was looking forward to seeing Betty. We had found out a few weeks before that she was pregnant with our first child and we were both very happy. When I got to the apartment, Betty and I talked about how we spent our day. Having gone to visit her friend, Eleanor, she told me that Eleanor and her husband Marty were having some serious problems because Marty did not like his job. He was working as a writer for a large public relations firm and disliked having to enhance the lives of people he did not even know.

Betty told me she mentioned to Eleanor how I was trying to make a living peddling. When Eleanor asked whether I liked what I was doing, Betty didn't know how to answer her. I thought about the question for the first time. With our growing family, making a living was my main concern; it overshadowed any other consideration by far. I told Betty that despite all the lousy jobs that I had held in the past, if I could make any decent money at peddling, I would love it. I told her I had purchased some more glass balls and that the next day, which was Sunday, I was going to Orchard Street, and felt I would do well.

At this point, our conversation took a slightly different turn. Betty started talking about how she had always wanted a family life and a man who was what she called a "homebody." She became emotional and started talking about how I was now too involved with what she referred to as "my new job." I felt hurt and tried to explain that we were going to need money, since she was now pregnant. Having a child would be a big expense. After all, neither of us had any savings.

I began to feel dejected, because the person that I considered to be my partner did not seem satisfied. Yet I didn't feel depressed, as had happened so often in the past. My new endeavor was providing me with a sense of direction and purpose, even if it was non-traditional. As we retired for the night, I felt a sense of apprehension between us, but the law of nature soon took hold and life was back on course.

The next morning after breakfast in a local coffee shop,

I asked Betty if she wanted to walk me over to Orchard Street. I had about twelve boxes of glass balls and I wanted to transport six of them by hand on the dolly. I loaded the cart and we left the house at about 10 a.m. With Betty along side of me keeping me company, I enjoyed the feeling of camaraderie as we walked along Houston Street, with its large tenement buildings, dilapidated yet livable. We turned into Orchard Street and walked to the corner of Orchard and Delancey Streets, where we stopped briefly to observe the conditions.

Delancey was a long business street near the Williamsburg Bridge leading to Brooklyn, lined with stores of every kind above which were apartments, giving the feeling of a live marketplace. Delancey Street had a pulse that gave real meaning to commerce. Orchard Street, which intersected Delancey, had a similar tempo, with smaller stores and buildings very close to each other. Delancey was a somewhat more traditional commercial environment while Orchard Street had a more Old World bazaar atmosphere.

A keen eye could discern a class difference in how the shoppers carried themselves and dressed, almost as if some of the Delancey Street shoppers would not lower themselves to set foot on Orchard Street. I opted to assert my democratic spirit and set up on the corner of the intersection as the shoppers arrived, many with large families carrying or wheeling their infants. As the street became congested with shoppers, I could see several peddlers hawking various items. Betty said that she wanted to take a walk for a while, so I was left to concentrate on my little world.

I wasn't selling at a very good pace and was beginning to think more about the hats that I had seen the prior day. After about an hour and a half, Betty came back and we talked a bit. She spoke in an animated tempo, buttoning and unbuttoning her pea coat, which was getting slightly tight around the waist. As she talked she took little steps back and forth like a peacock. She mentioned that she had seen a couple of people selling glass balls. This explained the mystery of why I wasn't doing as well as I had planned. I began to realize that as the Christmas holiday neared, there would be much more competition on seasonal items made just for the holidays. Betty asked me to take the rest of the day off, which didn't take much coaxing.

As we walked home to put the goods away, I felt frustrated. I knew the time was right to make some money, but I felt I needed a stronger item. At home, we had lunch and then went to the movies.

The next morning I went to the wholesale hat market at 32nd Street and Broadway. Looking around in a totally amateurish way, I felt as if I was groping for a large object in my immediate path, almost stumbling over it but unable to get hold of it. I saw some stores with signs saying they were wholesalers and that they spoke foreign languages. I was shy about entering, but realized I had no alternative.

The first store I went into was large and narrow, with a man and woman who appeared to be husband and wife seated at a counter. They were both plainly dressed, unlike the people I had met in the garment industry while working as a shipping clerk. The woman at the desk scrutinized me carefully. I had been sized up before, but never so thoroughly. I felt as if I was getting the total once-over.

When the woman asked what I was looking for, I described the hats that I wanted to buy. She abruptly said that she did not have them and seemed to be uninterested in doing business with me. I asked if she knew who might have the hat I was looking for. She shrugged and said, "Look in the directory and see what you can find in the building."

The directory listed several hat outlets. Each of the places I entered in the building had similar setups. Some companies took up an entire floor, while others occupied one space among many. Some of the offices had a receptionist and some did not, but someone would always come to the front entrance and ask what they could do for me. When I explained the type of hat I wanted to buy, they generally asked where my store was located. Once I told them I was a street peddler, they would either smile and say that they didn't have anything or ask me to come back to the factory, always located in the rear of the loft.

At the fourth place I went to, I saw a bald-headed, big husky guy who looked like he weighed around three hundred pounds surrounded by boxes of all shapes and sizes. He had a jovial manner, and asked why I didn't get a regular job. I asked him if he would pay me five hundred a week if I worked for him. At that point, he laughed so hard that the yarmulke he was wearing fell to the floor. Eventually I got around to telling him what kind of hats I was interested in buying. I explained that I had recently started peddling. He began to show me hats that he said I could buy from him at a reasonable price, but they were not the hats I was interested in. We got into a discussion on why I thought that these hats would not sell as fast as the ones that I had seen. I was on very shaky ground, since he was in the business and I was a novice.

It was obvious that he did not have what I wanted and was trying to sell me what he had. Some of the hats he showed me seemed neat and stylish. He even offered to take them back if I could not sell them, but I refused. I knew if I could locate the hats I was looking for, I would have a sure winner. I thanked him and was preparing to leave when he picked up a notebook and glanced through a few pages. He stopped on one of the pages, took a pencil and wrote a name for me, saying this man might have what I was looking for. I thanked him for his time and lost no time in going down to the place he had directed me, located at Bond Street and Broadway in lower Manhattan.

When I arrived at the building I had a hard time finding the entrance. I finally located it around the corner. After I rang a bell, a man in traditional orthodox Jewish dress came down a flight of stairs. He asked me what I wanted and seemed a bit apprehensive as I explained that I was a peddler and was interested in purchasing hats. He gave me a thorough sizing up before pointing to an old set of cast iron steps that led to a lever-operated elevator, which he skillfully handled. When we reached the third floor, he opened the elevator and we stepped directly into the factory, which was operating in full swing. I noticed a long cutting table and bolts of the faux fur that the hats I was looking for were made out of. There was lots of noise from the sewing machines and the dust began to fill my nostrils.

The workers were mostly black and Hispanic women. I had not been in a factory of this type since my childhood when visiting my father. The place gave me a feeling of nostalgia. I was very happy when I saw Itche, the owner, smiling and holding the hat I had been looking for as he walked back from the stock and shipping room at the back of the shop.

I did not want to act overly eager, so I nonchalantly asked the price of the hats. He explained that these were just a few of the hats he was currently making and that if I was interested he would show me more styles. I agreed to look at more styles, wanting to give the impression that I was still shopping and had other options. After a few minutes of stalling, I asked the price of the style I originally wanted. Looking me straight in the eye with a warm smile beaming through his thick beard, Itche said the price was $13 a dozen. I took this as a challenge to bargain and said I would start off with him by taking 20 dozen at $10 a dozen. He chuckled and asked if I was "mishuga."

I answered him in my best Yiddish, learned as a boy from Mrs. Dorfman in Brooklyn. We had a short conversation where I gave a slightly different spin to some of the events that were happening in my life, like that I was married to a nice Jewish girl, which was not the case. I was living with a nice girl who like myself didn't follow any religious ritual. Settling on a price of $12 a dozen, I took 10 dozen to start.

It was now about two weeks before the holidays and I realized that I could sell anywhere that I observed crowds of people. As I set up and sold, I noticed that my best customers were working women who wanted to purchase a decent gift for a friend or maybe for themselves. Outside large office buildings were always good spots for selling ladies items. I tried to stay clear of other peddlers who had similar items.

I secured my old Ford with a stronger portable trunk lock. The car came in handy, but I did get several parking violations, as well as summonses for selling in restricted areas, which added to the cost of peddling and cut into my profit.

I continued to buy from Itche, despite the fact I was hearing about other suppliers through the peddlers' grapevine at the Horn and Hardart's cafeteria, where I was becoming a regular. It seems that no matter how busy the season, how intense the trade, or how turbulent the conditions, there was a hard core of street merchants who always found time to hang out and exchange their divergent philosophical and economic ideas, picking the minds of their colleagues, which could better be called street research.

As the days wound down and the holidays neared, I was already about $1,500 ahead of where I had started seven weeks before. One fact and one fact alone disturbed me: I kept hearing about the "bean season," a time after New Year's when everything was slow and you couldn't even sell beans on the street.

Christmas and New Year's came and went. I think I wanted to believe the stories I had heard about not being able to do business again until March. Although peddling was the most profitable thing I had ever done, I did think about trying to find a more traditional way of earning my living. I was feeling guilty about being involved in what I considered to be a somewhat mercenary endeavor. I did not like the idea of having to constantly search for my next move. What's more, I was looking for more excitement and less stress; a difficult combination to fulfill in real life.

Betty and I were spending more time together as her pregnancy progressed. We went for short car rides, saw movies, and ate in a lot of inexpensive restaurants. We were having a hard time getting along with each other. I think that we were basically both insecure people who needed more structure in our lives than either of us could provide for the other. I felt a strong love for Betty, but never really had confidence in our relationship. When I tried to analyze the arguments we were having, I could never figure anything out. Maybe if we had had more economic security, things might have been better.

Betty and I both shared in the importance of the moment and we both wanted to be good parents. Around the second week of January, I began feeling restless and decided that I would go out and try to peddle to see for myself how things would be. I took all of the 12 dozen hats that I had left over and went to a spot where I thought I might be able to do some business. As things turned out, it was so slow it was not worthwhile being out.

After I got back home and unloaded the car, I took a walk over to the restaurant to see if any of the guys were around. Seeing several familiar faces, I sat down at one of the tables with a guy named David, a tall, fast-talking fellow with a quick smile. I remembered meeting him on Nassau Street and Maiden Lane in the Wall Street area one afternoon about a month before. I had set up on the corner just before the afternoon lunch break when he came along and told me I had to move because he was paying for this spot. I hadn't known exactly what he meant, but since it was pretty busy anywhere you looked, I located another corner with no trouble.

When we got to know each other, I casually recounted that incident to him and asked him what he meant when he said he was "paying for the spot." He told me there was a person downtown in the precinct called a bagman who picks up money from the peddlers. This made it easier to work the busy spots. The picture began to come together a little more, since I remembered being ticketed while a peddler next to me was not bothered at all. As we chatted, I mentioned to him that I had been out and found things very slow. He said that the only days worth working this time of the year were paydays because most people were broke, and even then you needed a real strong item. This made sense to me.

The next Friday afternoon, I went out again and stayed on the spot I had chosen for about four hours. After receiving two tickets for peddling in a restricted area and selling about two dozen hats, I became disappointed and left. Actually, I had not done badly for the time of year, but I had become spoiled and was not interested in what is known as "grinding," which means making money slowly. I had been bitten by the fast money bug and wasn't going to settle for a slow day's pay. If I wanted that, I could always go back to waiting on tables.

When I got home at around 10 p.m., Betty said that staying home alone at night was scary, especially now that she was pregnant. I said that I would try to stay home and keep her company more often. We talked for a long time that night and decided on two things: We would get married in the near future before our child was born, and we would get a dog the next day.

The next morning we went to a pet shop on 14th Street and looked the dogs over. We decided that a German Shepherd would be a good choice and found a two-month-old female puppy that looked nice. We paid $175 for her, took her home and fed her a good meal. She was friendly and very smart. She was no trouble to paper train and soon became housebroken. We named her Maymie.

The next two weekends, I sold the rest of the hats out, and was satisfied with the profit after expenses, but I needed something during the week. I dreaded going back to waiting on tables, but knew I had to do something during the slow season. The next week I swallowed my pride and went to the waiters union. Jack Shimell was still the labor chief who assigned the work. He always was in good humor and interested in the union members. He asked me where I had been for the past couple of months and I explained that I was trying a business on my own. I described it as selling apparel at worksites and explained I needed something to carry me through. He assigned me a weekend job in a fish place at Sheepshead Bay in Brooklyn and told me I could work something out with the shop steward if I wanted to continue to work during the week. We shook hands and I wished him good health, as he was quite old and had suffered a stroke the year before.

Waiting tables seemed more boring and dull than ever before. I felt as if I had died and been buried in this place. The money wasn't bad, but it was nothing compared to what I knew I could make if only I could get the right item for the street. I was becoming frustrated. It was as if there were several ropes in front of me and I didn't know which one to grab onto to pull myself up out of the hole I was in.

Feeling not too sure of myself and having a lot of spare time, I began feeling very insecure. I hadn't seen my friend, Ken, for a while and decided to call him and see how he was doing. I also had respect for his judgment and thought this would be a good opportunity to get his advice. We agreed to meet at Union Square Park, since it was a nice day and we could sit and talk. I arrived first and within a few minutes, I saw Ken walking toward me with a bag of coffee and donuts.

As we sat and chatted, Ken was getting a big kick out of some of the things that I was experiencing. We discussed some of the political events that were happening, like the war in Vietnam and the protest movement against it. I was not very politically active at the time, but was still on the mailing list of the Veterans for Peace. As we spoke, I began to focus more on Betty, who was now in her 4th month of pregnancy. I began to visualize what I wanted out of life at the time. I began to fantasize about a family and a home with love and some of the creature comforts that had always seemed out of my reach. I felt myself becoming animated and emotional because I was expressing plain ordinary basic desires that I had never been able to express – not even with Betty. When I tried to talk to her about plans for the future, she would become emotional and we would both feel uncomfortable.

As I spoke with Ken, ideas were forming in my head. I began to realize that peddling was my only salvation and that I would have to commit myself more than I had in the pre-Christmas season, which was an easy time to sell. I decided with some input from Ken to start operating on a larger scale. To do this, I needed an enclosed van, which I decided to buy with part of the money I had saved up.

After a while, I looked at my watch and realized that we had been sitting and talking for over three hours. We were both hungry and went to a local Chinese restaurant for lunch. After lunch, Ken said I could call him if I needed help finding a second hand vehicle to use for work. I said I would check the newspaper and probably give him a call in the next few days. The following morning I bought several newspapers and looked at the offerings. An advertisement for an auto and truck auction at 10 a.m. the following Saturday at the New York City Department of Sanitation caught my eye. I noted the time and place and asked if Ken would join me at the auction, I was plunging head first into a real business and needed all the advice I could get.

Chapter 18: A Good Day For Umbrellas

Ken and I were at the Sanitation Department car and truck auction bright and early on Saturday morning to inspect the vehicles. A 1964 International Travellall panel truck that had been used as an ambulance caught my eye. I started it up and drove it about six feet forward and six feet back, all that was allowed during the pre-auction inspection hour. This truck had only an astonishing 13,000 miles registered on its odometer and I didn't think it had been turned back. I saw a couple of other people looking at this vehicle and knew that there would be some bidding competition. One guy even told me that he operated a small children's school bus service and that he liked the vehicle because it was clean. When this truck came up on the bidding order someone opened it at $350. I bid $5 or $10 higher each time and eventually noticed that at about $500, only the bus operator and I were in contention. We advanced our bids $10 dollars at a time. At $550, he advanced me only $5 to $555. In an act of what I considered to be bravado, I advanced the bid by $10 while giving the guy a quick glance, and listened as the gavel came down three times, making me the proud owner. I went up to the desk, gave my deposit, filled out the necessary papers and made an appointment to pick the truck up Monday morning.

When I arrived Monday morning, I paid the remaining balance and took possession of the vehicle. I was not expecting it to be perfect and in driving felt a pull to one side of the road which I recognized as a front end problem.

I felt a lot better after I drove into a front-end alignment place on 14th Street and was happy to find out all I needed was a minor wheel alignment. After leaving the garage I took the car on a test drive on the East River Drive and was impressed with how easily it handled.

I placed a "For Sale" sign on my old car and had no trouble selling it to a guy who lived in one of the buildings on my street, since I had priced it fairly. Every time he saw me, he thanked me and told me how much his family was enjoying the car.

I had made a serious investment in a business and had to start operating. My job now was to find a marketable item. I became seriously committed to finding an item that I could work with until the spring arrived. I looked around the streets and noticed the peddlers working. I took notice of one guy who was known to be particularly unfriendly to people he did not know. He had a reputation for carrying an iron bar and would not hesitate to use it. I saw that he had a large truck filled with umbrellas of all kinds, which he unloaded onto a large hand wagon and pulled to the corner where he worked. I observed him during the afternoon, and although it was not raining he seemed to be selling a lot of the new folding-type umbrellas. After one lady purchased an umbrella, I saw her rip the label off and throw it to the ground. I walked behind her, swooped it up and read the company name on it.

I went to the building where the company was located on 32nd Street, entered and walked toward the factory section, avoiding the office. There was a long table where several men stood assembling handles on the umbrellas. A middle-aged man came over and asked if he could help me. When I told him that I wanted to buy umbrellas to sell in the street, he said that he did not sell to peddlers. I answered that I had a veteran's license and that I wanted to buy. He still objected. I told him with a slightly raised tone that I had seen people selling his umbrellas in the street. After some verbal sparring, he agreed to tell me the prices and show me his line of merchandise. I bought an assortment of men's and ladies' styles based on his recommendation. I figured that since I did not know anything I might as well put some trust in this guy, since we now had some kind of an understanding. I suspect he realized I would make a good customer, despite his general apprehension over doing business with peddlers, or maybe he was just using reverse psychology.

I loaded the goods into my new vehicle for which I'd secured a commercial license plate from the Department of Motor Vehicles. With commercial plates, one got fewer tickets, since commercial vehicles were subjected to less stringent rules. I had my small wagon in the truck and headed directly for 14th Street and Broadway, my home turf.

It was a bright sunny day. Though I had not observed people buying umbrellas in this kind of weather, I believed it could happen. As soon as I set up, people began coming over and showing a great interest in the folding umbrellas. I soon learned that this was a very hot item. I could make a good day's pay with it any day and a super payday when it rained. Rather than always working on 14th Street, I began to move around and learn where the good spots were.

There were days that I took in as much as $500. At 33% profit, that wasn't bad in 1969. Occasionally, I would meet Morris who carried the iron bar at some of the spots. We sort of respected each other and got along all right as long as we didn't work the same corners.

An apple peddler who was known as a 'conditions man' collected for the police in the Wall Street area, which was in the first precinct. His apple cart was on Wall and Williams Streets. The apple peddler was mainly in the numbers business. He picked up numbers sheets from runners in the nearby buildings, usually elevator operators, which he turned over to his boss. The level of organization was beyond my imagination. I would have never believed that this low marginal level of underworld activity existed had I not been in the midst of it.

Each time I went to the downtown area, it was like entering a dream world. The uniform police were mostly Italian, Irish, and Jewish-American Old World types, each a character in his own way. They would appear regularly to write summonses, which we all knew were part of the operating expenses. I paid income and some sales tax regularly each year, since we were all compelled to register with the Department of Consumer Affairs.

Those who got on the wrong side of the conditions man and were not paying regularly were referred to as outlaws and their goods were confiscated until they appeared in court and paid a fine. The good boys who paid off regularly could gather fifty or a hundred summonses over a period of months and before a warrant was issued for a peddler's arrest, a warrant officer would send word out that he wanted to see the peddler. He would then find a friendly judge and clear all of the tickets for $1 apiece. When the peddler went in to pick up the tickets, they were usually stamped fifty cents each. These activities were not practiced by all of the officials involved, but there was enough corruption at the time for a full-scale investigation. The 1973 Knapp Crime Commission, and the later Maurice Najari Commission, were established to investigate corruption in city government. During these investigations the heat was on us peddlers and it became more difficult to operate.

One day when I had just finished working the morning rush and was putting the goods back into the truck, a police car with two cops pulled up alongside and asked to speak with me. I recognized one of the cops, who wore sergeant stripes, as a guy assigned to the peddler's detail. I walked up slowly to the car and stood by his window as he spoke. He knew my first name and began talking in a very friendly and casual manner.

He started talking about how policemen who want to make the higher ranks had to take courses at John Jay School of Criminal Justice. Beginning to feel uneasy, I asked why he was telling me this stuff. He looked at me, smiled and said in a commanding tone, "Stanley, you are a fucking recidivist." I asked in a respectful manner what a recidivist was. "It means, Stanley, that when you come from wherever the fuck you come from to this precinct you always peddle your shit."

At this point I interrupted and said, "I sell quality merchandise". But he continued, "And when I give you a ticket, you just don't give a fuck and you come back again and again and again." He went on to explain that other guys who come to peddle never come back after they get a ticket, because they are not recidivists.

I broke my silence and said I had to make a living to support my family. Again he smiled and said, "I'm glad you said that, Stanley, because that's just what I wanted to hear. You see, we have to make a living, too, and you know there are some people who are called investigators going around and asking a lot of fucking questions about things that are happening down here, and some of the peddlers are talking too much and telling a lot of fucking lies. So, Stanley, I know that you are going to use your good judgment. Right?"

I nodded in agreement and the conversation turned to whether the Yankees were going to clinch the pennant. I never heard any more about it. As always, the heat blew over and we went back to the same old payoff game.

Although peddling activities were far from a main source of corruption, they figured prominently in the Knapp proceedings. Nothing much was uncovered. I was not called to testify, but a friend of mine recounted how he had been met by two official-looking gentlemen who flashed impressive gold badges and asked a bunch of questions. He told me they asked if he knew anything about stolen goods that were being sold around the city. He said he was not aware of any and left it at that.

I had heard there were many truckloads of goods being hijacked, especially around the airport and waterfront truck routes. Stolen goods, called "swag," were sold by people who hung out in various social clubs around the city, usually in Brooklyn. This stuff did not interest me, because I was buying merchandise from a couple of legitimate wholesalers at good prices.

I don't know what I would have done if I had been questioned, but I knew the problems that our country was encountering in Vietnam were much more serious than peddling corruption. I had taken part in some of the protests and felt part of the peace movement. I wished I could give more time to the anti-war movement, but I had to work long hours to support my family.

As far as I was concerned, I didn't have the emotional stability to hold down a 9 to 5 job. I don't know why, but seeing the boss making so much money and me not even having enough to buy a pair of shoes at the end of the week had always been a source of depression for me. I was happy not to be in that position any more.

One rainy morning after working the morning rush on

Park Avenue South in front of the Metropolitan Insurance building, I saw another peddler I knew, Little Joey, a short, pudgy guy with shifty eyes, just as I was getting ready to pack my stuff into my truck and go to have breakfast. Little Joey was like so many of the people in my life, an addicted gambler and a sometime peddler who worked in the downtown area. Little Joey had done a year on Rikers Island for burglary.

As he walked up to me to say hello, I noticed that he was wearing a sweatshirt with blood on it. He appeared to be very weary. A few guys who had worked with him in the past had said they always made money working with Joey, but they didn't trust him. Since I was going to breakfast, I invited him to join me for some coffee and eggs. We went to the Bellmore Cafeteria, a joint I liked to eat at ever since I had driven a cab a few years back.

As we ate our coffee and eggs, I wanted to ask Joey where the blood on the sweatshirt came from but refrained. I mentioned that I hadn't seen him for a while. Joey explained that he had been operating a small store in downtown Brooklyn, but there had been some trouble with his partner and now he was broke. He mentioned who his partner was. I knew the man was a Brooklyn wise guy who went by the nickname of Mike the Hammer and had done time for manslaughter. Joey said Mike had bankrolled the store as an 'absent partner'.

Joey said he had just come from a night in the hospital. Looking at his bloodstained sweatshirt, it was safe to assume he had taken a beating. As our talk progressed, he admitted that he had had a bad losing streak betting sports and had wound up in a fight with Mike. Joey also mentioned that his wife had thrown him out of the house.

After we finished our breakfast and were walking back in the direction of the truck, Joey told me about a wholesaler down on Orchard Street who had panty hose at a good price. He asked me if he could keep his 'joint' in my truck. Seasoned, old-time peddlers referred to their street vending operation, their setups and goods, as their 'joint'. I wasn't doing very well at the time, plus I figured Joey had burnt out all his contacts. But against my better judgment I said I'd help him until he got back on his feet. Besides, I felt lonely since I had no one to talk to during the day.

We drove down to a wholesaler where Joey managed to get some goods from the guy on credit. Joey and I then drove downtown to set up for the lunch time rush in the financial district. No fool, Joey set up near me because he knew he could work on my patch, thanks to my police 'connection.' As things went, neither one of us did much business. While we worked together for another few days, I heard all about the one-year bit he did on Rikers Island for burglary, a lot of his Navy stories from the Korean War and a lot of his capers from the past.

Joey was a fast talker. Somewhere in between all his talk, he told me about a manufacturer we might make some serious money with. He called and made an appointment with the guy. Believing I had nothing to lose, I said I'd go with him to see this Larry at his factory in the garment district on lower Broadway. When we got to the lobby of the building, we were asked by the security guard who we wanted to see. We told him "Larry" and he directed us to the 4th floor.

When we got up to the 4th floor, a young woman who introduced herself as Iris asked us who we wanted to see. Joey explained that he had done business with Larry in the past and we wanted to see him. As she took us to his office, Iris told us that Larry was her father and that she was now in the business with him.

As we walked toward his office, I noticed that the factory looked clean, with nice machinery in full operation, just like the place where my father had worked in New Jersey, but much bigger and with many more machine operators, cutters and pressers working at a pretty fast pace.

When we got to the office, Joey and Larry immediately recognized each other. Joey played the big man in the operation. He didn't even bother to introduce me, even though we both knew I was the one with the money to buy the goods, the truck and the police connections. I went along with this script, feeling in the long run I could make some real money in the deal.

After another few minutes of small talk, Larry said he would show us around. He took us to a section where finished garments were hung on racks. Joey and I examined the merchandise closely. The boat neck, cowl neck and V-neck garments with cap sleeves, short sleeves and long sleeves had various well-known designer labels, which led me to believe they would be very expensive and out of our price range. When Larry told us the prices, I knew they had to be knockoffs, but didn't ask.

I put up the money to buy goods that day. We continued to do business with Larry on a regular basis. As a matter of fact, his shirts were made of very good cotton and had embroidered logos, better than the stamped logos that I had seen on much higher priced designer goods.

We bought these shirts for $4 each and sold them for $6, priced to sell fast. The retail stores were getting a much bigger markup, which gave us a pretty good edge. We borrowed racks from Larry. The shirts sold faster than we could bag them. The garments had union labels, the customers were happy, Larry and Iris were happy and we all felt we had a good deal.

On most days, we made good money. We usually worked midtown for the morning rush, trying to avoid the police as much as possible since we were working with a lot of goods and my connections weren't strong in the midtown 17th precinct. It wasn't the expense of the summonses as much as the fact that they were time consuming because all selling had to stop while the police wrote out the tickets. The lunch hour rush downtown was the real strength of the day. We had a good working relationship with the police in that precinct and weren't bothered with tickets. We went downtown for the evening rush.

A couple of times, the police told me to come to the precinct house to pick up my summonses, their way of covering themselves. A couple of times when I had my five-year-old son, Greg, with me, one of the cops showed him the horses in the police stable located next to the precinct on Franklin and Varick Streets. The little guy had a great time and I think even learned a little about life in New York City.

My old friend Doolittle used to say, "You got to make hay while the sun shines." I took that seriously and worked long days peddling.

Before long, Joey got back on his feet and was doing okay with me. Even though when I counted the goods, the count usually came up on the South side, I was thankful that he had turned me on to the item and didn't make an issue of what I considered to be an operating expense.

About a year after we were working together, Joey's daughter met a guy who wasn't working, (and I don't think had ever worked). Joey decided to make him a peddler. I went along with it for a while. We did a three-way split, but it didn't work and we decided to part company. I started to work on my own again. Years later, I ran into Teddy Fowler, another peddler who pitched slice-and-dice machines right in the street. Teddy asked if I was still working with Joey. When I told him Joey and I had split up, he said, "He probably didn't want to work with you anyway – you count the goods."

During this period, two brothers began peddling designer shirts with a different approach. They rented a small loft and employed people to sew logos on the finished garments. The mistake they made was duplicating the designer logos exactly, thereby opening themselves up to copyright law violations. When I told Larry of their operation, he only had one thing to say. "What fucking crooks!" Iris said, "People like that should be in jail." I had to stop myself from laughing, thinking Larry and Iris might have been serious. Actually, Iris was supplying the brothers with the shirts that they put the knockoff logos on.

About six months after the brothers started their cottage industry, they were both busted on a misdemeanor charge, given a stiff fine and a warning by the judge. I never found out what the charge was. I do know they continued to work as if nothing had happened, until one of the brothers was busted about six months later. This time the charge was a felony "violation of copyright code." He copped a plea and served a year in Attica.

As time went on, several guys asked to work with me. I never really wanted a big operation in the street, but eventually gave a few guys goods to sell. A couple of them had police records and were finding difficulty getting jobs. I trusted them and overall found them to be good workers.

Chris, a new guy who had just completed a drug rehab program, started to work with me. I had to build a rack like mine for Chris to put the goods on. It was my original design, with the helpful suggestions of a guy in the plumbing supply store where I bought the poles, elbows and flanges for the rack. The moving rack was similar to the one I had made when I started to sell designer sweaters.

It wasn't until I left my apartment at 6:30 am and began wheeling my platform rack with bars that I also found out the bars could be used as weapons. Since I couldn't get the rack down the four flights of stairs from our apartment, I had to carry the bars separately, which was difficult. I placed the bars on the plywood platform and pulled it with a rope.

As I pulled the small platform display rack with the bars on top to my van parked down the street, a couple of the bars kept rolling off the small hand truck, making a big noise at that hour of the early morning. I almost got to where my van was parked when a shirtless guy ran out of his apartment building and picked up one of the bars, which was quite thick, and raised it over my head. I pushed up and, as he pulled down, I pushed down in the same direction until getting to his knee height and pulled him. He fell and lay splattered on the sidewalk.

As he tried to get up, I held the bar and told him not to move. He said he was cold. I thought of giving him my jacket, but it wasn't that cold. I did let him sit up. At that point, people were looking out of their windows. A woman said she had called the police. After a few minutes, the police and EMS came. When they asked me what happened, I pointed to the guy on the ground and explained. Lucky for me, the guy did not deny my statement. EMS took him to the hospital.

As the EMS vehicle left, the two cops who had been called were in a discussion. I heard one say "Ain't you gonna take him in, Timmy"? Timmy answered, "The other guy came at him with the bar." After taking all my information and identification, Timmy gave me his number and told me to call him before he got off his shift at 3 o'clock.

When I finally got through to him that afternoon, he told me the guy had been drunk, didn't live in the house ,was shacking up and was dismissed from the hospital unhurt. I knew the guy was not hurt because I had not hit him hard. I didn't know that he was drunk and felt sorry about the whole incident. I should not have been making so much noise so early in the morning, but you gotta make a living.

On one occasion, a peddler friend of mine discussed some of the harassment taking place at the time. He mentioned that if we are asked to get a license to peddle, why should we be getting so many tickets for violating laws that no one could even find on the books? I didn't see a few tickets as a problem, but some of the other guys did.

We formed an organization, collected enough money to get a good lawyer by the name of Ed Posner, and brought charges, including harassment, against the City of New York. I was one of four military veterans named in the lawsuit to end the harassment. The case was eventually mediated in the office of a long-time judge. The police agreed to stop arresting peddlers and impounding their goods, sometimes even taking them away from those who had a patch or were on the pad, that is, were paying the police off.

The agreement reached was that the police would require peddlers to move to another spot. This was pretty good, because another spot in the same vicinity could not be much different. Everyone felt the agreement would be impossible to enforce, which it was. The advantage was that it bought time for the peddlers and we did well for the year that this agreement lasted.

All through the years there have been laws, agreements

and many forms of harassment for street peddlers. Nothing has ever worked for long because peddling is a tradition in New York going way back. Besides, it's an honest way to make a living. Mayor Ed Koch argued that since the store owners were paying high rents, it wasn't fair for peddlers to work and not pay rent. I believe he knew what was going on with the payoffs but played dumb for political reasons. If storeowners were willing to be gouged for unreasonably high rents, that was their problem.

That was old New York before everything from upscale watches to toothpaste were knocked off and pirated in from overseas. As manufacturing moved from lower Broadway to outside the United States, Larry and his daughter eventually moved their operation to Costa Rica. The street got hot for peddlers. I began thinking it was time to try something new.

What I would do next was anybody's guess.

Chapter 19: Family Life

As Betty approached the ninth month of her pregnancy, I was gearing up for the next fall season. Since I had been doing pretty well, I decided to take a few days' break as the day of our child's birth was nearing. Betty and I went for rides and walks and spent those days doing things together. Although we were experiencing problems in our relationship, the act of becoming parents together seemed to create a magical sense of warmth and sharing that was like no other emotion I have ever had.

When Betty and I left the hospital with our son, Greg, bringing him home in the taxi was a deeply memorable experience for both of us. We just kept looking at him and looking at each other and smiling. Reading Dr. Spock had been our only preparation for parenthood. He was not only the childrearing guru of the day, but had run for president on the Peace and Freedom ticket.

We were very proud to have such a handsome, healthy baby. I was especially happy since I had taken a lot of ribbing from friends, telling me that they hoped the baby looked like Betty and not me. I was beginning to think that some of them weren't kidding.

The homecoming with our beautiful baby took place two weeks before a large peace demonstration was scheduled. I felt that I needed to attend this event and march with the Veterans for Peace contingent, as I had done in the past. I was sharing in all the household chores and was doing as much as I could to make things easier for Betty.

Yet I also understood that Betty was not accustomed to

Stan, Betty and Greg

being alone with our child. I offered to accompany her to her friend's house and promised that I would only be gone for a few hours. She did not want this and an argument erupted. My feeling at the time was that I needed to go to this demonstration not only for the future of my newly arrived son, but for all of the children of the world. We finally came to an agreement that she would call to see if her friend Emily could stay with her and the baby for the afternoon. Emily came downtown and I said I would call every hour, which I did, even before cell phones.

I have come to doubt the wisdom of my action on that day, but, at the time I did not believe I could have behaved otherwise. When I returned home, Betty was still angry, but we did talk it out. I do not think she ever got over the hurt. I know I never got over the guilt. This episode in our relationship taught me that there would be no easy answers and sometimes no solutions.

About a week later I went back to work. I continued with the same types of items and life became business as usual. The newness of peddling was wearing off and it was becoming something of a grind. The only difference between this and other things I had done in the past was that I was making more money now and had more control over my life. That, combined with the fact that I had to support my new family, kept me going.

I made the acquaintance of a guy named Paddy O'Shea.

Paddy had been hustling on the streets and eventually bought a medallion cab but never really got the street life out of his blood. Whenever I met him, he would ask me if I were going to work "this doing" or "that doing." At first I didn't know what he was talking about when he referred to these "doings." I soon found out that "doings" were events like parades, where hustlers would sell items like flags and pennants to the large crowds that turned out. Peddlers who worked these "doings" usually would drive long distances, some even going as far as New Orleans for Mardi Gras. I worked a few local "doings" but didn't feel too comfortable pinning a small American flag decal on a guy's lapel at a Veterans Day parade, putting my hand out for a quarter or sometimes a buck contribution while snapping off a neat salute. As the in gag went, "two salutes for a buck." I always got a big kick out of hearing Paddy's stories, but this just wasn't my thing.

Shortly after our son was born, Betty became pregnant again. We decided that we needed more room and moved into an apartment in a private house in the Red Hook section of Brooklyn, a quiet working class community. I was hoping for a girl and the following March, our daughter Nina was born just one day before Greg's first birthday. Nina was healthy and beautiful, high-spirited and lovable.

Around this time, Betty seemed to be getting overburdened, and I did not know what to do about it. I tried to be more helpful, but felt that I had to be out making money. I arranged to pay our neighbor's daughter to help Betty, but it was not enough. Almost anything could trigger one of our frequent arguments. I began to feel helpless and a failure. The thing that I wanted most in life was a happy family, but it seemed that was not going to happen. It was as if my work was a waste of time. It was becoming obvious that what I wanted most, a close family, was unattainable.

Betty and I talked about getting help through counseling, but it never happened. I kept on working, which for me was an outlet, while Betty was stuck at home with the kids, very unhappy.

We did go to places like zoos and parks on weekends, but it felt as if we were just going through the motions. The real ingredients were not there and there were no substitutions. I felt that no matter what I did and how much love and affection I showed, nothing was working. When the kids reached their 2nd and 3rd birthdays, we found a good day care center and Betty took a job in Manhattan as a secretary. I thought that her working might turn things around but it didn't. She told me that she wanted to start dating and we had to break up.

At first I thought she was not serious. I figured I was either dreaming or not hearing correctly. I was shaken out of my state of denial when she told me that she was seeing somebody she was working with. My mind began working overtime in all directions. I didn't know what to do or what to think. Every time we started to discuss what was happening, we wound up in an argument. I hated for the kids to see this and was surprised at how much they grasped and understood about what was happening, even though we tried not to talk in front of them.

It had become a nightmare. I often had to stop and think to realize that this was really happening. When I looked at the kids, I saw them growing up with a single father from a broken marriage. The thought terrified me. I did not know what to do. Desperation was taking me over.

As I stayed home at night with the kids when Betty was out, I began to think of bad things. I was not a violent person, but the desperation of the moment was beginning to make me despair. I had a pretty good idea of who her boyfriend was and thought of doing him physical harm. The only thing that stopped me was, I couldn't be sure who the man was, and I didn't want to make a mistake. The idea of seeking revenge became an obsession. I thought about everything from a beating to a more serious type of attack. Eventually I realized that this was not the answer and would only make things worse.

Betty informed me that she was leaving temporarily – without the children – and would return in about a week. Then we would have to find a solution. I felt as if my world was coming to an end and the walls were closing in on me.

Each morning the kids asked for their mommy. I didn't know what to say. I told them that she was on vacation. It was a hot summer. On one of the days their mother was gone we went to a swimming pool. Our daughter, Nina, seemed not to have been as affected as Greg. He was three at the time and she was only two. As he came out of the water, he asked for his mother and I made some excuse. At this point, he broke into tears and I felt as if my body was in a vise. I felt miserable and ashamed.

After a few days, Betty called and said she was returning the following Sunday. I let the kids talk to her and saw how happy they were. Despite all of my anger toward Betty, from my own childhood experiences, I realized how important a mother is in the lives of children. Betty's short absence and our children's reaction helped me to better understand what I had gone through as a child, growing up separated from my mother.

When Betty came home on Sunday night, the kids were very happy to see her, as was I. But it felt like a reunion was taking place and I was not invited. Betty and I agreed that she would stay in the apartment with the kids and I would leave. It hurt. Hurt bad. I stayed with a friend in

Manhattan for about a week before finding a cheap apartment on the Lower East Side. The kids visited me regularly as I adjusted to my new life.

On one occasion, after about a month, Gregory mentioned something about Frank, who I knew was Betty's boyfriend. A short time later I found out they were living together. I asked the kids almost every time we were together if there were any problems at home between them and Frank. They always said that things were okay. We agreed that if they had any problems, they would speak to me. I kept working the same as before and made an agreement with Betty to pay child support, since we had no formal arrangement.

As far as peddling, I was now doing a lot better since, in the mid 1970's, there were a lot of goods around in various warehouses in Brooklyn that could be purchased at a good price, but I always was careful about who I dealt with.

Chapter 20 Moving On

Sometime around 1975, Betty asked if I would pay for an uncontested divorce and I agreed. I paid child support and saw Greg and Nina as often as I could. I was feeling pretty bad about my family's breakup and wanted to find something 'more respectable' to do with my life. I started hanging out with Ray, a friend who was taking night courses at the New School of Social Research on 12th Street.

Sometimes I attended a few of the classes with him. I found some of them interesting, especially when issues of social justice were being discussed. I wanted to take part in the discussion and felt I knew as much as the students, but I didn't talk, which was hard for me to do. After class, Ray and I went to drink beer at the Cedar Tavern, one of the popular Greenwich Village watering holes. It was dark with heavy wood mahogany fixtures, a pre-World War II décor and a lot of drunken artists at the bar.

One time Ray's girlfriend, Ruth, who often hung out with us, mentioned that she had a teaching job at a place called Touro College, which had just opened a new branch on 44th Street between 5th and 6th Avenues in New York City. She was very enthusiastic about her new job and talked about how Touro was part of a new concept in education. She explained how the college had an adult life experience program and gave college credit to people for their work experience. I was immediately interested and asked her if Touro had a co-ed program. She and Ray got a big laugh out of my question. I went to find out more about the program the next afternoon.

As I walked into the lobby of the building I noticed several young men carrying books and wearing traditional Orthodox and Hasidic black outfits. In an office with a glass enclosure, a man inside motioned for me to come in and offered me a seat. I asked how I could find out more about the adult program which I had heard about. He handed me some written material and asked if I had any questions. I asked what the eligibility requirements for getting into the program were. He answered, "Don't worry."

I asked if my GI bill as a Veteran was acceptable and what tuition would be covered. I got another, "Don't worry." I asked again if the courses were difficult and he said, "They are important and educational and on a very high level but not overly complicated." I asked how soon I could enroll and he said I could fill the papers out now and start very soon. I was happy but wanted to learn a little more about the program. I said it sounded good and I would come back to enroll after reading their material.

When I got out in the street I called Ray from a pay phone and explained where I had been. I said it would be nice if Ruth, he and I could meet and discuss my enrolling in the Adult Life Experience Program at Touro. We met at the Cedar for dinner that evening. After finishing our food, I showed Ruth some of the information I had on the courses. She looked them over with interest, since she was scheduled to start teaching two courses in the next week, but didn't know yet what she would be assigned. As she looked at the curriculum she smiled and began reading some of the course descriptions out loud: Freedom and Commitment, Life and Identity: Bridging Cultural Differences: Examining the Cosmos, and Changing Times. She laughed and said, "This stuff sounds challenging." I agreed, puzzled at the fact that she didn't seem to know much about Touro's curriculum.

When I asked them whether I should enroll, Ray said, "What do you have to lose, Stan?" I went the next day and chose two, six credit courses for the next semester, which was to start the following week.

As I had been told, Touro was part of Yeshiva College. It had orthodox Jewish students during the day session. In the evenings, it converted to the Adult Life Experience Program, which was attended at the time by mostly minority men and women students who were highly motivated and were willing to make sacrifices to get an education.

On the first session of Freedom and Commitment, there were about ten students in the class. The room had nice chairs and was well painted and large. I thought how funny it would be if Ruth were my teacher, but the Professor was a young man who said he taught during the day at Fordham University. After we introduced ourselves the Professor made a few jokes to loosen things up and then passed out a list of books. We were to read at least two of the books during the semester. He then said he would give a short lecture on what the content of the course would be and that we should take notes. We would be able to refer to our notes during a discussion that would happen after the lecture.

His lecture dealt with committing ourselves to hard work and the benefits that could be derived from dedication to good values. I found parts of the lecture interesting, but at times felt as if I was back in the Quaker meeting that I once attended. Anyway, I participated in the discussion and was glad to have an opportunity to share some of my ideas.

A short time before the end of that first session, the

Professor asked whether any of the students had long distances to travel, like to the Bronx or Brooklyn. Since some did, he dismissed the class a little early, but not before asking whether we liked our session. We all said we did. He said he looked forward to our next meeting and that we should start our assigned reading. I left the class glad to be part of my new college environment.

As time went on, I learned that many of the professors were well-respected on their day teaching jobs and also understood the special situations of their evening program students.

One gentleman, a man of color who was very well-spoken and always dressed immaculately, taught Changing Times, a course that I enrolled in. He began his lecture by explaining that he had served in Vietnam and earned a First Lieutenant field commission. After being discharged, he was promoted to the reserve rank of Captain. This was just around the time of a scandal that had taken place at West Point Military Academy where cadets were being given special consideration during tests. After completing his lecture, he stated that he was going to give the class an essay test using the honor system and that he would leave the room, "just like at West Point."

A short time after the test began, one student asked how a word was spelled. Since she was sitting near me and I considered myself a pretty good speller I complied with the spirit of the test and told how the word was spelled. When the papers were graded and given back the next week I noticed that she had earned an A on the paper and I had a B. I asked to read her paper. It was really good. I think I should have been asking her for help.

As I continued to peddle I developed more of an interest in my college work. I was taking about 20 credits a semester and enjoying the open environment and friendly interaction. I also was part of a committee that we formed to help students get better Pell grants. We were successful in getting several of our students help, which made it easier for single people with families to attend classes.

The high point of the night was our after class campus hangout at Nathan's hot dog joint on 6th Avenue. I found our get-togethers great fun and always looked forward to them.

So for me, Touro was a natural place to be. I also met several nice women who were attending the program. Between college, business, my kids, and my social life, I had neither time, nor reason to be depressed or feel sorry for myself. It was as if my life had been restructured, and it wasn't half bad.

After earning 100 credits in course work and completing a required Life Experience paper (about seven pages long), I qualified for my Bachelor's degree in Psychology from Touro College. I attended the graduation and felt proud of my accomplishment. Although I had better feelings about myself, my day to day life hadn't changed much. I kept on hustling merchandise on the spots that I'd built up over several years and just kept doing what I had been doing.

One hot, steamy summer evening, while sitting in Blimpies on 12th Street and 6th Avenue in Greenwich Village, one of the local air-conditioned hangouts, my friend, Charlotte asked me whether I was ever going to do anything with my college degree. She told me about a program she had read about in the New York Times. Because of a teacher shortage in the area of Special Ed, the New York City Board of Education was offering the teaching position to inexperienced candidates. Applicants had to bring a copy of their college transcript to the Board of Ed to be accepted into the program. The applicant would then take 6 credits in Special Education at New York University during the summer session, which was starting in one week. Those who qualified would be given a job teaching Special Education at the beginning of the fall semester.

As I thought about the prospect of becoming a teacher, I found it was something I wanted to try. I went through the program with no problem and was invited to what was called a "hiring pool," which took place on the ground level of an old school building in Brooklyn. There were several tables with one or two people sitting behind each one with a sign saying: Elementary Schools, Middle Schools, and High Schools. There were short lines by the tables of people waiting to be interviewed. Thinking high school would be a good place to start, I got on that line.

When I got to the front of the line the interviewer informed me that only Bushwick High School in Brooklyn was available. I said I would take the job. No questions were asked and I was given the day, time and place to report for work.

I got to Bushwick High School early, where I met the supervisors and some of the teachers. I was asked to fill out some papers before an orientation for new teachers was to take place. After completing all of the formalities of the first day, I said goodbye to a woman who I was sitting next to in the auditorium. She bent over and told me to be careful when leaving because this was a "very bad neighborhood." I got home safely that day and every day for the three years I taught at Bushwick.

When Monday morning came, I reported to the office of the Special Education supervisor and was told where my home room would be. I was also given a list of courses I would teach and a roster of students and their evaluation levels. These evaluations were given by the committee of officials who had placed the students in Special Education.

I taught math and science. The students were difficult for me to handle. I did not have any experience at teaching. After a few weeks, I told the supervisor how I felt about the whole matter. He told me that my students were the most difficult and I should just do my best to help them.

I enrolled at the City College of New York in a Masters of Education Program and found that most of the other teachers had the same problems in their schools that I was facing. I completed the Masters program in two years and got my degree, but I didn't see much of a change in my classroom situation.

All teachers were required to have lesson plans for each class session, but I was never able to get through the lesson because of the many discipline problems I encountered in my classes. When I tried to discuss the problems with the students, they told me they were bored.

This has made me believe that many of these youngsters would do well in settings where academic work was combined with productive activity. Most of my students were past the age of 18 and were in good shape. Many of the young men and women could have made excellent construction workers, but our system doesn't work for them.

What worked best for me was when I felt I could not complete the lesson, I allowed people to express why they were acting out. Often what I heard were real grievances. I tried to make lesson plans which dealt with some of the problems they expressed. Nothing seemed to work, and after a period of time my attitude became very negative.

At first, I blamed myself and felt that someone else could do better. After a period of time, I realized that I was just helping to warehouse youngsters with problems. I resigned from the job after "teaching" for three years.

Having a civil service job with a strong union was beneficial for me because it gave me a feeling of security. I did want to do something where I felt I could make a contribution and make a difference in the lives of people who were in need. After a few days off, I applied for a job at the Department of Social Services. I was hired on a temporary basis until the next test for caseworkers was given. I was assigned to work at the Fort Washington Men's Shelter, which housed as many as 1,200 single men and was located in an armory on 168th Street and Broadway in Manhattan.

Working in shelters gave me an opportunity to provide services for folks in need. I was thankful to be able to help them at a time when they needed support. I helped place Vietnam Veterans in a shelter that had just opened in Long Island City where they could get special help and, in many cases, their own apartments. The subject of our homeless problem and other problems is not often written about because it makes people feel uncomfortable, but if conditions are ever to be improved it's going to have to take a lot of productive thought and a whole lot of hard work.

I worked for the shelter system as a shift supervisor until my retirement in 1995.

After a stint of retirement time and some travel, exercise, a lot of film and theater, it dawned on me that I was bored. A college teacher friend told me that Hudson County Community College had some openings in the English department. So I applied for an adjunct instructor position. After a short interview, I was given classes to teach that were called Academic Foundations. I would be teaching students who did not yet qualify for college matriculation because of language problems.

To be frank, what they really needed was someone who had a degree in Teaching English as a Second Language. But not wanting to pay the price for one of these highly skilled professionals, the College hired me for less money.

My job was simply to get the students to where they could read and understand one paragraph and be able to write one paragraph on a given subject. I did not grade the test papers at the end of the semester. That was done by a committee. If the students achieved a passing mark they would become matriculated and were given the credits for all the subjects that they had previously completed. They would be able to graduate when the time came.

On the side, I worked with the American Federation of Teachers to organize adjunct instructors at the College. The organizing drive was successful and we won our election. The conditions of adjunct instructors improved, but not enough. I was ready to move on. I was offered a job teaching introductory sociology. This was an area I was more interested in. I also felt that I had done all I could do at Hudson County Community College.

I taught sociology at Berkeley College on 44th Street in New York City. There is a Berkeley in California and a Berklee Music School in Boston, but I think the New York City school may be the most interesting. It was imbedded in several office buildings in Midtown Manhattan. I often had to walk up several flights of stairs and run to another building to make my class on time, which was why the Chairperson who hired me had asked me how good I was at climbing stairs. The aerobics gave me a complete workout.

The students attending Berkeley College came from

many different countries and must have had a lot of money judging from the New York City living expenses and tuition they were paying. I don't think they took sociology too seriously, but a good time was had by all. Rumor had it that it would be easier to win on the lotto tickets that they were constantly scratching than to get a failing mark in my class.

After two years of teaching at Berkley, my wife and I felt our New York life style was getting too expensive. We moved to western Massachusetts.

Having lived in big cities most of my life, the western New England life style does have a lot to offer: beautiful outdoor scenery, great history, nice progressive people and affordability. After living here for the past 9 years I am sure I will get used to it by the time I am 100 years old.

Chapter 21: Last Trip To Florida

Some questions should never be asked – they might be answered.

As a child I was not comfortable being critical of my father – the person who was putting food in my mouth. Dependency is a subtle form of victimization and can lead to a feeling of helplessness in a child. As I grew up, I sometimes doubted the credibility of this man who as my father was my natural role model. In the past, whenever I have felt myself about to trip over an old wound dating back to this part of my childhood, I have been able with a great deal of effort to stuff the bad memories down deep inside me and focus on the more pleasant side of life. But some questions nag at you. They weigh on your mind until you feel you just have to pursue them.

I made the last visit to my father in Florida when he was 93 years old. I was 55 at the time and hadn't been down to see him in ten years; maybe more. What was the point? Since he was never going to enlighten me about all the family mishegoss from my childhood years, why bother confronting him now?

Because deep down in my gut, I still wanted to know why the marriage had been so chaotic and violent, and I wanted to know how my mother died. Maybe Pop wouldn't give up anything new, but if I didn't try, I'd forever kick myself for letting the opportunity slip through my fingers.

So I flew down to Florida, grateful to have my wife Sally with me, and not knowing it would be the final visit.

He died seven years later at the age of 100.

On a cool Spring morning, we arrived at the Orange Blossom Nursing Home in Hollywood, Florida, where my Pop lived. Pop's third wife, Stella, had passed away six years before, so I knew he was really alone. The last time Sally and I had seen him was in 1981 when Stella was very sick. I liked Stella, although I never got to know her well, and I was sad to learn of her death in 1983.

When we entered his room at the nursing home, he looked us over as was his style when meeting people. He shook hands with me with a grip as strong as when I was a kid and gave Sally a nice hug.

As we sat together in the dining room of the home, I evaluated the situation and concluded that this was a good time to talk. He had just finished a breakfast fit for a lumberjack: eggs, hot cereal, tea, and a Danish. I thought we might have to take a break to give him a nap, so I asked, "You want to take a nap Pop or do you want to still talk?"

He just looked at us in his usual style and quipped, "For big shots talk is work, for me it's recreation; I can talk."

The man was still sharp. I knew the only way to ask this question was to put it out early in the discussion and make it shortly worded. I was anxious to get to the point once and for all and I had confidence that he could handle the situation.

I approached him not as a loving son seeking acceptance from his father, but more as a predator hunting for an elusive truth. We sat across from each other at a little table, he not saying anything. He lit a small cigar, coughed into a wad of tissues and dropped it on the table.

"Why were things so difficult when you and my mother got back together after your breakup when I was a small boy, Pop?"

He stared at me with a look I hadn't seen since I was in foster care and about 12 years old, when we were living in Brooklyn. On that night, he came to the basketball courts where the kids used to hang out and saw me smoking a cigarette. I don't remember where I got the cigarette, but I do remember the two smacks in the face that he delivered with an open hand and the startling sting and embarrassment that I experienced in front of the other kids.

But this day was many years later and his guard was down. In response to my question he cracked a sly grin and said, "You vant me to tell you? Your mother vas no good. I never should have married a divorced woman. She didn't know how to manage money and she vas crazy. She used to bark at me like ah dog."

I had heard him make this accusation about her barking often during their arguments, but, as I remember it, his tirades and physical abuse were over the top and scary. I thought he was hypocritical, since he had a gambling habit and was always short of money, a situation that increased the tension we all felt. I do remember Kate talking about how well other members of our family were doing, like my Pop's brother or her father, and I know this really got to Jake's ego big time. When they argued he would often push her against the kitchen wall or the refrigerator. It made me cry and feel as if I was lost.

When he told me the same old bull shit story, I became uneasy and angry. I could not drop it. Maybe I should have let the matter go, a lot of sons would do that. After all, he was now a very old man and we were going back a long way. An inner voice kept saying, "Drop it, drop it, you have nothing to gain, nothing will change," but I couldn't just leave it alone. Maybe sometimes the best closure might be no closure, but I still had questions and I still wanted answers, and in no way was I satisfied.

"I know times were hard Pop: the Depression, a lot of mouths to feed on a tailor's salary and all that, but you both were pretty bad and went at each other a lot."

"You were a baby" he said, "Vat do you know?"

"I remember, Pop. It hurt me and I remember."

I could have told him how I remembered him hitting her hard during one of their fights, and how I went into my room and cried at the time, but I didn't.

Sometimes it seemed that I might have just dreamt all this stuff. Children have colorful imaginations, maybe it wasn't all that bad. But the broken dishes my father threw around the kitchen – I didn't make that up. And I didn't make up my Pop pushing my mother around on a regular basis.

"Remember my mother, Kate, Pop?" He shook his head up and down. "How did she die, Pop? Was she choked"?

No answer.

"My grandfather said she was choked, Pop. Julius said he called the police on you."

No answer. No expression on his face. He just took a swig of coffee. We looked at each other intensely. Silently. After a few seconds he shook his head from side to side and said, "She ate something on her trip with your sister the day before."

I still couldn't help looking at those big strong hands and visualizing the damage they could do: to cut through thick leather and sew thick cloth; to battle young Russian anti-Semites in the sea town of Odessa, Ukraine; maybe even to strangle or smother with a pillow a 43 year old woman with serious emotional problems.

And where was my Grandfather in all of this. Why didn't he push for a full investigation? He did call the police, but why didn't he press the issue with the District Attorney? Was it the financial expense he would have incurred? Was it a matter of shame or embarrassment? He must have cared about his daughter. I regret never having had this discussion with him.

One time I did bring the question up of our mother's death when my half-brother, Julius, my mother's son from her first marriage, came to visit me and Betty in Brooklyn. When I asked him why our grandfather didn't push for an investigation, Julius said he did push, at first, until the District Attorney told him an autopsy was needed for an investigation to be ordered. Julius said that our grandfather was of the belief that autopsies were a desecration and forbidden by Jewish law. My opini0n was that our Grandfather was a small businessman and didn't want the bad publicity. Neither Julius nor I were happy about how it ended up with no investigation, but we both dropped the issue at the time. Besides, it happened so long ago, there was no way for us to open any kind of investigation so many years after the event.

I remembered Pop's temper; how it would flare, like the time he fought the boss in the factory where he worked and head butted him, giving the guy a bloody broken nose. I know my mother often brought up the fact that a lot of other people were making more money than my father while he gambled away their money, and I know that hurt him.

I remembered how he threw the dishes, smashing everything in sight, cursing my mother, pushing her and chasing her out of the room.

Now here he was, seated across from me. His eyes were still defiant, but the rolling waves of fury had receded. He was a lonely old man. When Stella was alive he was more affable than I had ever known him to be, but now with her gone he seemed distraught and unhappy. I hadn't visited him for a few years and I don't think Meyer or Hymie did either. We were more a family in name than in fact.

It occurred to me that he might even have mixed up what happened that terrible day in his own mind. Pop had always been good at twisting the truth to suit his devious intentions, like the way he blamed his father-in-law for losing the house when grandfather wouldn't loan him any more money, when it was Pop's gambling that drove us down into debt and shabby rooming houses. Maybe he'd twisted the truth up so much, he couldn't tell me the facts about my mother's death even if he wanted to.

At that moment I did feel a bond with him. He was my dad, he did some good things and he did some bad things. Who was I to judge him?

I turned to Sally, my wife and my best friend. She put a hand on my arm, indicating she knew what I was thinking. Pop had nothing more to say; I had no more questions to ask.

When we left him that day I told Sally I felt good about the meeting. She asked me what I meant. I had to think long and hard on the drive back to our hotel before I could put it into words. What I finally came up with was, there are mysteries in the world that we will never uncover. We have to figure out what questions are worth asking and asking until we get the answer we want, and which answers will always escape us.

After much thought I decided that Pop deserves at least the benefit of the doubt. After all, here we were, two old men who I am sure felt we had both made a lot of mistakes in our lives and it was too late to change any of it. At this point it was all about acceptance and forgiveness and leaving some questions unanswered.

Finding happiness ... finding peace of mind – those are goals that we have to reach for every day, and we can't let the unknown parts of our lives drag us down into despair. I have a loving wife, a good family, work, friends and memories. The past is like a cemetery; we can visit if we want or we can abandon it and let the weeds grow. But whatever mysteries lie beneath those headstones, we can't let them kill our dreams.

I guess I learned that lesson late in my life. Learned it the hard way.

I hope my Pop learned it, too.

Epilogue: It's Where You're Going

I was just talking to a guy recently. I don't remember his name, but I remember him saying, "It's not where you come from, it's where you're going that counts." I guess this has stayed with me because of where I came from – a dysfunctional family right from the beginning, social and economic problems

Stan Maron

all screened by a maze of denial and a stream of confusion hanging over my head well into my adult life. I don't remember having any clear direction, but I always tried for something better than what I was experiencing and was willing to work for it, if I could just find out what it was.

In my early years, I did what I could to survive, like bussing dishes and waiting tables, followed by day labor secured in sleazy employment agencies. I hustled pool and three-cushion billiards until I volunteered for the army in 1954. After an uneventful two-year tour of duty in the Army, I was discharged in 1956, once again not really knowing which way to turn.

So I did what came naturally and picked up where I had left off. I tried selling in many forms from the garment industry to door-to-door canvassing, but nothing seemed to work until I started peddling on the streets of New York City. Peddling seemed to fit my emotional makeup and

I made pretty good money at it. I was my own boss and was able to set my own work structure without too much outside interference.

In later years I found fulfilling jobs in social service and education. It was in working to help people who were less fortunate than others that I began to think more about the obligation we all have to make the world a better place for all.

Gradually having a little more financial and personal security made it possible for me to focus more on where I was headed. I met interesting people, some of whom had a social justice agenda, which gave me a new way of seeing things and a new way of confronting life.

I confess meeting new people, a happy relationship and a good family hasn't made me the happiest guy in the world, but I feel a whole lot better than I did for most of my life. I attribute that to many of the people I have come in contact with and the support they have given me in my adult life. I'll finish by saying if I'm not the happiest guy in the world, and I'm not, it's because I just want too much! The experiences of my early years, which I wouldn't wish on anyone, may have provided me with the ability to stay in the game and keep my spirits up even when I felt I was going against targets moving faster than I could keep up with.

TITLES FROM HARD BALL PRESS

The Lenny Moss Mysteries, by Timothy Sheard

THIS WON'T HURT A BIT
SOME CUTS NEVER HEAL
A RACE AGAINST DEATH
SLIM TO NONE
NO PLACE TO BE SICK
A BITTER PILL

HARD BALL PRESS Standalone Books

LOVE DIES, A Thriller, by Timothy Sheard

MURDER OF A POST OFFICE MANAGER,
A Legal Thriller, by Paul Felton

SIXTEEN TONS,
An Historical Novel, by Kevin Corley

*WHAT DID YOU LEARN AT WORK TODAY? THE
FORBIDDEN LESSONS OF LABOR EDUCATION*,
Nonfiction, by Helena Worthen

WITH OUR LOVING HANDS
1199 NE Nursing Home Workers Tell Their Story,
edited by Tim Sheard

MANNY & THE MANGO TREE
Ali & Valerie Bustamante

30841464R00166

Made in the USA
Middletown, DE
09 April 2016